Pastor Tim's CleanLaugh Collection

Printed in Victoria, Canada

National Library of Canada Cataloguing in Publication Data

```
Davis, Tim, 1965--
 Pastor Tim's cleanlaugh collection
ISBN 1-55369-030-3
1. Canadian wit and humor (English)   I. Title.
PN6178.C3D345 2001    C818'.602         C2001-903457-1
```

TRAFFORD

This book was published *on-demand* in cooperation with Trafford Publishing.
On-demand publishing is a unique process and service of making a book available for retail sale to the public taking advantage of on-demand manufacturing and Internet marketing.
On-demand publishing includes promotions, retail sales, manufacturing, order fulfilment, accounting and collecting royalties on behalf of the author.

To order more copies in any quantity go to
www.cybersalt.org
or e-mail:
bookorders@cybersalt.org

Dedication

To all who have
ever made me happy
by laughing with me,

Thank You.

Why I Can Laugh

The world is very often not a funny place.

Every day someone's life comes down around them after loosing their job, getting bad news from their doctor, losing a love or loved one close to them, or something else momentous that happens to tear the fabric of the life they have woven.

And as I have learned only recently, it seems that each generation becomes afflicted by sorrow that stems out of something they never imagined could happen - something they will be destined to bear in their minds for as long as they draw breath.

And yet, the world still laughs.

Some laugh to forget while others do so to mask their pain. Still others laugh hoping that the emptiness of their soul will somehow be filled by merriment and cheer. I would like to share with you why I can laugh.

On November 4, 1965, I made my grand entrance into the world at the "keeper weight" of 10 pounds, 1 ounce. Six months later I was diagnosed with cancer (bi-lateral wilms tumors). Doctors removed the two tumors (one the size of a large grapefruit and the other a small football) along with half of each of my kidneys. Next came 28 radiation treatments that left me an ashen gray color and with a pronouncement that I had 3 months to live.

God had other plans.

At least that is what I was told by my mother growing up. Countless times she would remind me, "Tim, you weren't supposed to live. God has a plan for you." Her ongoing reminders bred a deep enjoyment of life into me and an ongoing awareness that there was a God.

It wasn't until I was thirteen though, that someone showed me in the Bible that my just believing that God existed, and my living of a relatively good life, would not be enough to get me into Heaven. For the first time I saw that imperfection could not exist in the presence of the Perfect God.

I was shown that God had a sure remedy for my and mankind's dilemma. God entered into our world in the person of Jesus Christ, to live a perfect life and die a perfect sacrifice to remove the guilt of our past, present, and future life in this world.

Truly, this makes great sense. For when one thinks of it, how can living a good life undo the hurt our sins have done to others and ourselves? Having become imperfect, how can one ever regain perfection by that means? The best season of the best baseball player cannot overcome the negative effect of past poor seasons on his lifetime average. It may improve it, but perfection can only be attained by the reapplication of absolute perfection from somewhere else.

And so, the Bible tells us, in the fullness of time, Jesus came and bore the sins of the whole world so that through faith in His sacrifice for imperfect sinners, His perfection could be counted as theirs, indeed given to them by God the Great restorer and reconciler Himself.

What does that mean to you and me? Well, we don't have to slug it out in a fruitless effort to cover over the troughs and valleys of our past. We don't have to pretend all is ok and always has been, in a vain attempt to trick God at the end of time. Gone are nights of wondering what eternity will hold, and so too days that are fraught with scary reminders of the seeming vanity and hopelessness of life.

Because of Christ, and more importantly in Christ, our souls are set free to live this current life for God and make the most of what this world sometimes scarcely offers us. Even as mankind rejects God we can reject mankind's rejection of Him and know Him personally. Come what may, Jesus Christ makes all the difference in this life and the next.

That's why I can laugh.

Pastor Tim

October 2001

3

WWW.CYBERSALT.ORG

There's lots more clean jokes,
pictures, videos, and sounds at:

www.cybersalt.org/cleanlaugh

Surf on by and check them out and while you are there
you are invited to subscribe, for free, to one of
Pastor Tim's e-mail lists.

Plus, if while you are reading later, you end up
wondering what a Goober is,
you'll find a good picture of one at:

http://www.cybersalt.org/cleanlaugh/goober

Bachelor Cooking

Two confirmed bachelors sat talking. Their conversation drifted from politics to cooking. "I got a cookbook once," said the first, "but I could never do anything with it."

"Too much fancy cooking in it, eh?" asked the second.

"You said it. Every one of the recipes began the same way - 'Take a clean dish and....'"

Play Quietly

Donald MacDonald from the Isle of Skye (or maybe it was Neil McNeil from Barra, but anyway) went to study at an English university and was living in the hall of residence with all the other students there. After he had been there a month, his mother came to visit him (no doubt carrying reinforcements of tatties, salt herring, oatmeal and whisky).

"And how do you find the English students, Donald?" she asked.

"Mother," he replied, "they're such terrible, noisy people. The one on that side keeps banging his head on the wall and won't stop. The one on the other side screams and screams all night."

"Oh, Donald! How do you manage to put up with these awful noisy English neighbors?"

"Mother, I do nothing. I just ignore them. I just stay here quietly, playing my bagpipes."

Free to Go

John and Timothy were in an institution. This place had an annual contest where they picked two of the best patients and asked them two questions. If they got them correct, they were deemed cured and free to go.

John was called into the doctor's office first and asked if he understood that he'd be free if he answered the questions correctly. The doctor said, "John, what would happen if I poked out one of your eyes?"

John said, "I'd be half blind."

"That's correct. What if I poked out both eyes?"

"I'd be completely blind." The doctor stood up, shook John's hand, and told him he was free.

On John's way out, as the doctor filled out the paperwork, John mentioned the exam to Timothy. He told him what questions were going to be asked and gave him the answers.

So Timothy came in. The doctor went through the formalities and asked, "What would happen if I cut off one ear?"

Timothy, remembering what John had said, answered, "I'd be half blind."

The doctor looked a little puzzled, but went on. "What if I cut off the other ear?"

"I'd be completely blind," Timothy answered.

"Timothy, can you explain how you'd be *blind*?"

"My hat would fall down over my eyes."

Differences Between Men & Women

NICKNAMES:

If Gloria, Suzanne, Debra and Michelle go out for lunch, they will call each other Gloria, Suzanne, Debra and Michelle. But if Mike, Phil, Rob and Jack go out for a brusque, they will affectionately refer to each other as Fat Boy, Godzilla, Peanut-Head and Useless.

EATING OUT:

And when the check comes, Mike, Phil, Rob and Jack will each throw in $20 bills, even though it's only for $22.50. None of them will have anything smaller, and none will actually admit they want change back. When the girls get their check, out come the pocket calculators.

BATHROOMS:

A man has five items in his bathroom - a toothbrush, shaving cream, razor, a bar of Dial soap, and a towel from the Holiday Inn. The average number of items in the typical woman's bathroom is 437. A man would not be able to identify most of these items.

GROCERIES:

A woman makes a list of things she needs and then goes out to the store and buys these things. A man waits till the only items left in his fridge are half a lime and a soda. Then he goes grocery shopping. He buys everything that looks good. By the time a man reaches the checkout counter, his cart is packed tighter than the Clampett's car on Beverly Hillbillies. Of course, this will not stop him from going to the 10-items-or-less lane.

SHOES:

When preparing for work, a woman will put on a Mondi wool suit, then slip on Reebok sneakers. She will carry her dress shoes in a plastic bag from Saks. When a woman gets to work, she will put on her dress shoes. Five minutes later, she will kick them off because her feet are under the desk. A man will wear the same pair of shoes all day.

CATS:

Women love cats. Men say they love cats, but when women aren't looking, men kick cats.

DRESSING UP:

A woman will dress up to: go shopping, water the plants, empty the garbage, answer the phone, read a book, get the mail. A man will dress up for: weddings, funerals.

LAUNDRY:

Women do laundry every couple of days. A man will wear every article of clothing he owns, including his surgical pants that were hip about eight years ago, before he will do his laundry. When he is finally out of clothes, he will wear a dirty sweatshirt inside out, rent a U-Haul and take his mountain of clothes to the Laundromat. Men always expect to meet beautiful women at the Laundromat. This is a myth perpetuated by re-runs of old episodes of "Love, American Style."

OFFSPRING:

Ah, children. A woman knows all about her children. She knows about dentist appointments and soccer games and romances and best friends and favorite foods and secret fears and hopes and dreams. A man is vaguely aware of some short people living in the house.

The Senior Driver

As a senior citizen was driving down the freeway, his car phone rang. Answering, he heard his wife's voice urgently warning him,

"Herman, I just heard on the news that there's a car going the wrong way on 280. Please be careful!"

"Mabel," said Herman, "it's not just one car. It's hundreds of them!"

Old Dodge

A man was driving along in his beat up old dodge, when suddenly it broke down. He was parked on the side of the road trying to fix it, when a Jaguar pulled up in front of him and offered to help.

After a few minutes the two men obviously weren't going to get the old car going again, so the Jaguar driver offered to tow the Dodge to the nearest garage. A few minutes later the two had hitched up the old Dodge to the Jaguar, and they agreed that if the Jaguar driver was going too fast, the man should blow his horn and flash his lights to get him to slow down. With that the two men got into their cars and the Jaguar driver started to pull away with the Dodge behind it.

At the first traffic light, a Ferrari pulled up beside the Jaguar and started to rev his engine. As soon as the light turned green the Ferrari and the Jaguar hit their accelerators and took off. Before long the cars were racing at over 120 mph.

As the cars sped along, they passed through a police speed trap. The officer couldn't believe his eyes when he saw the three cars go by, and he decided that he couldn't catch them all by himself, so he radioed for help: "You won't believe what I just saw! A Ferrari and a Jaguar are doing 120 mph side by side, with a beat up old Dodge behind them flashing his lights and blowing his horn trying to get by!"

Poor Preachers

After the church service a little boy told the pastor, "When I grow up, I'm going to give you some money."

"Well, thank you," the pastor replied, "but why?"

"Because my daddy says you're one of the poorest preachers we've ever had."

Keep on Walking

An eight-year-old boy is walking down the road one day when a car pulls over next to him.

"If you get in the car," the driver says, "I'll give you $10 and a piece of candy."

The boy refuses and keeps on walking.

A few moments later, not to take no for an answer, the man driving the car pulls over again. "How about $20 and two pieces of candy?"

The boy tells the man to leave him alone and keeps on walking.

Still further down the road the man pulls over to the side of theroad. "OK," he says, "this is my final offer. I'll give you $50 and all the candy you can eat."

8

The little boy stops, goes to the car and leans in. "Look," he says to the driver. "You bought the Ford, Dad. You'll have to live with it!"

The Lord's Prayer – sort of

A mother was teaching her three-year-old The Lord's Prayer.

For several evenings at bedtime, the child repeated it after the mother. Then one night the child was ready to solo. The mother listened with pride to the carefully enunciated words, right up to the end.

"And lead us not into temptation, but deliver us some e-mail, Amen."

Interesting Thoughts

Why do we say something is out of whack? What is a whack?

If a pig loses its voice, is it disgruntled?

When someone asks you, "A penny for your thoughts," and you put your two cents in, what happens to the other penny?

Why is the man who invests all your money called a broker?

When cheese gets its picture taken, what does it say?

Why is a person who plays the piano called a pianist, but a person who drives a race car not called a racist?

Why are a wise man and a wise guy opposites?

Why do overlook and oversee mean opposite things?

If horrific means to make horrible, does terrific mean to make terrible?

Why isn't 11 pronounced onety one?

"I am" is reportedly the shortest sentence in the English language. Could it be that "I do" is the longest sentence?

If lawyers are disbarred and clergymen defrocked, doesn't it follow that electricians can be delighted, musicians denoted, cowboys deranged, models deposed, tree surgeons debarked and dry cleaners depressed?

Do Roman paramedics refer to IV's as "4's"?

Why is it that if someone tells you that there are 1 billion stars in the universe you will believe them, but if they tell you a wall has wet paint you will have to touch it to be sure?

If people from Poland are called "Poles," why aren't people from Holland called "Holes?"

Share by Example

A mother was preparing pancakes for her sons, Kevin, 5, and Ryan, 3.

The boys began to argue over who would get the first pancake. Their mother saw the opportunity for a moral lesson.

"If Jesus were sitting here, He would say, 'Let my brother have the first pancake. I can wait.'"

Kevin turned to his younger brother and said, "Ryan, you be Jesus."

Dead Seagull

A father was at the beach with his children when his four-year-old son ran up to him, grabbed his hand, and led him to the shore, where a seagull lay dead in the sand.

"Daddy, what happened to him?" the son asked.

"He died and went to Heaven," the dad replied.

The boy thought a moment and then said, "Did God throw him back down?"

"Grace"ous Hosting

A woman invited some people to dinner.

At the table, she turned to their six-year-old daughter and said, "Would you like to say the blessing?"

"I wouldn't know what to say," the girl replied.

"Just say what you hear Mommy say," the wife answered.

The daughter bowed her head and said, "Lord, why on earth did I invite all these people to dinner?"

Gandhi Pun

Mahatma Gandhi walked barefoot everywhere, to the point that the soles of his feet became quite thick and hard.

Being a very spiritual person, he ate very little, and often fasted. As a result, he was quite thin and frail.

Furthermore, due to his diet, he ended up with very bad breath.

He came to be known as a....

"Super callused fragile mystic plagued with halitosis."

G.I. Excuses

The General went out to find that none of his GIs were there. One finally ran up, panting heavily.

"Sorry, sir! I can explain. You see I had a date and it ran a little late, I ran to the bus but missed it, I hailed a cab but it broke down, found a farm, bought a horse but it dropped dead, ran 10 miles, and now I'm here."

The General was very skeptical about this explanation but at least he was here so he let the GI go. Moments later, eight more GIs came up to the general panting, he asked them why they were late.

"Sorry, sir! I had a date and it ran a little late, I ran to the bus but missed it, I hailed a cab but it broke down, found a farm, bought a horse but it dropped dead, ran 10 miles, and now I'm here."

The General eyed them, feeling very skeptical but since he let the first guy go, he let them go, too. A tenth GI jogged up to the General, panting heavily.

"Sorry, sir! I had a date and it ran a little late, I ran to the bus but missed it, I hailed a cab but..."

"Let me guess," the General interrupted. "It broke down."

"No," said the GI. "There were so many dead horses in the road, it took forever to get around them."

Better by Train

A large two-engine train was crossing America. After they had gone some distance, one of the engines broke down. "No problem," the engineer thought and carried on at half power. Farther on down the line, the other engine broke down and the train came to a standstill.

The engineer decided he should inform the passengers about why the train had stopped, and made the following announcement: "Ladies and gentlemen, I have some good news and some bad news. The bad news is that both engines have failed, and we will be stuck here for some time. The good news is that you decided to take the train and not fly."

Dad's a Wimp

One summer evening during a violent thunderstorm a mother was tucking her small boy into bed. She was about to turn off the light when he asked with a tremor in his voice, "Mommy, will you sleep with me tonight?"

11

The mother smiled and gave him a reassuring hug. "I can't dear," she said. "I have to sleep in Daddy's room."

A long silence was broken at last by his shaking little voice: "The big sissy."

All Roads Lead Back to Rome
(How Specs Live Forever)

The U.S. standard railroad gauge (distance between the rails) is 4 feet, 8.5 inches. That's an exceedingly odd number. Why was that gauge used? Because that's the way they built them in England, and English expatriates built the U.S. railroads.

Why did the English people build them like that? Because the first rail lines were built by the same people who built the pre-railroad system tramways, and that's the gauge they used.

Why did "they" use that gauge then? Because the people who built the tramways used the same jigs and tools that they used for building wagons, which used that wheel spacing.

Okay! Why did the wagons use that odd wheel spacing? Well, if they tried to use any other spacing the wagons would break on some of the old, long distance roads, because that's the spacing of the old wheel ruts.

So who built these old rutted roads? The first long distance roads in Europe were built by Imperial Rome for the benefit of their legions. The roads have been used ever since. And the ruts? The initial ruts, which everyone else had to match for fear of destroying their wagons, were first made by Roman war chariots that were made for or by Imperial Rome. They were all alike in the matter of wheel spacing.

Thus, we have the answer to the original question. The United States standard railroad gauge of 4 feet, 8.5 inches is derived from the original specification for an Imperial Roman army war chariot.

Specs and bureaucracies live forever. So, the next time you are handed a specification and wonder what horse's rear end came up with it, you may be exactly right; because the Imperial Roman chariots were made to be just wide enough to accommodate the back-ends of two war horses.

Thoughtful Sidney

Sometime after Sidney died, his widow, Tillie, was finally able to speak about what a thoughtful and wonderful man her late husband had been.

"Sidney thought of everything," she told them. "Just before he died, Sidney called me to his bedside. He handed me three envelopes.

12

'Tillie,' he told me, 'I have put all my last wishes in these three envelopes. After I am dead, please open them and do exactly as I have instructed. Then I can rest in peace'."

"What was in the envelopes?" her friends asked.

"The first envelope contained $5,000 with a note, 'Please use this money to buy a nice casket.' So I bought a beautiful mahogany casket with such a comfortable lining that I know Sidney is resting very comfortably.

"The second envelope contained $10,000 with a note, 'Please use this for a nice funeral.' I arranged Sidney a very dignified funeral and bought all his favorite foods for everyone attending."

"And the third envelope?" asked her friends.

"The third envelope contained $25,000 with a note, 'Please use this to buy a nice stone.'"

Holding her hand in the air and showing off her ten-carat diamond ring, Tillie said, "So, do you like my stone?"

Stolen Goat

The following is a quote from a director of sports information in the Navy, regarding the theft of some mascots from the Naval Academy by army rivals:

"We knew army cadets were involved because they cut through two fences to get to the goats, and 15 feet away there was an unlocked gate."

Top 17 Inspirational Messages Not Heard At Work

17. There is no "I" in "teamwork"...But there is in "management kiss-up".

16. If you do a good job and work hard, you may get a job with a better company someday.

15. The light at the end of the tunnel has been turned off due to budget cuts.

14. Doing a job RIGHT the first time gets the job done. Doing the job WRONG 14 times gives you job security.

13. If you think we're a bad company, you should see the competition.

12. Rome did not create a great empire by having meetings...they did it by killing all those who opposed them.

11. We put the "k" in "kwality".

10.   2 days without a human rights violation.

9.   Your job is STILL better than asking, "You want fries with that?"

8.   We build great products when we feel like it and don't have any reason to call in sick.

7.   If at first you don't succeed, try management.

6.   Teamwork means never having to take all the blame yourself.

5.   The beatings will continue until morale improves.

4.   Pride, Commitment, Teamwork. Words we use to get you to work for free.

3.   If at first you don't succeed, delegate it.

2.   Plagiarism saves time...

And the #1 Inspirational Message Never Heard at Work:

1.   Eagles may soar, but weasels don't get sucked into jet engines.

Mr. Sugarbrown's Daughter

A certain little girl, when asked her name, would reply, "I'm Mr. Sugarbrown's daughter."

Her mother told her this was wrong, she must say, "I'm Jane Sugarbrown."

The Vicar spoke to her in Sunday School, and said, "Aren't you Mr. Sugarbrown's daughter?"

She replied, "I thought I was, but mother says I'm not."

Speeding Juggler

A driver was pulled over by a police officer for speeding. As the officer was writing the ticket, she noticed several machetes in the car.

"What are those for?" she asked suspiciously.

"I'm a juggler," the man replied. "I use those in my act."

"Well, show me," the officer requested.

So he got out the machetes and started juggling them, first three, then more, finally seven at one time, overhand, underhand, behind the back, putting on a dazzling show and amazing the officer.

Another car passed by. The driver did a double take, and said, "I've got to give up drinking! Look at the test they're giving now."

Helpful Executive

A young executive was leaving the office late one evening when he found the CEO standing in front of a shredder with a piece of paper in his hand.

"Listen," said the CEO, "this is a very sensitive and important document here, and my secretary has gone for the night. Can you make this thing work?"

"Certainly," said the young executive. He turned the machine on, inserted the paper, and pressed the start button.

"Excellent, excellent!" said the CEO as his paper disappeared inside the machine. "I just need one copy."

Last Words Heard

Three friends die in a car accident and they go to an orientation in heaven.

They are all asked, "When you are in your casket and friends and family are mourning you, what would you like to hear them say about you?"

The first guy says, "I would like to hear them say that I was a great doctor of my time, and a great family man."

The second guy says, "I would like to hear that I was a wonderful husband and school teacher who made a huge difference in the children of tomorrow."

The last guy replies, "I would like to hear them say... LOOK, HE'S MOVING!!!!!!!!"

Answering Machine Funnies

"Hi! John's answering machine is broken. This is his refrigerator. Please speak very slowly, and I'll stick your message to myself with one of these magnets."

"Greetings, you have reached the Sixth Sense Detective Agency. We know who you are and what you want, so at the sound of the tone, please hang up."

"Hello, this is Sally's microwave. Her answering machine just eloped with her tape deck, so I'm stuck with taking her calls. Say, if you want anything cooked while you leave your message, just hold it up to the phone."

"Hello, you are talking to a machine. I am capable of receiving messages. My owners do not need siding, windows, or a hot tub, and their carpets are clean. They give to charity through the office and don't need their picture taken. If you're still with me, leave your name and number and they will get back to you."

"This is not an answering machine - this is a telepathic thought-recording device. After the tone, think about your name, your reason for calling, and a number where I can reach you, and I'll think about returning your call."

"Hi, this is George. I'm sorry I can't answer the phone right now. Leave a message, and then wait by your phone until I call you back."

"If you are a burglar, then we're probably at home cleaning our weapons right now and can't come to the phone. Otherwise, we probably aren't home and it's safe to leave us a message."

"Hi. I am probably home. I'm just avoiding someone I don't like. Leave me a message, and if I don't call back, it's YOU."

How Cold Is It?
(An Annotated Thermometer)

(degrees Fahrenheit, then Celsius)

+50 / +10	New York tenants turn on the heat
	Thunder Bayites plant gardens
+40 / +4	Californians shiver uncontrollably
	Canadians sunbathe
+35 / +2	Italian cars don't start
+32 / 0	Distilled water freezes
+30 / -1	You can see your breath
	You plan a vacation in Florida
	Politicians begin to worry about the homeless
	Thunder Bayites eat ice cream
+25 / -4	Boston water freezes
	Californians weep pitiably
	Cat insists on sleeping on your bed with you
+20 / -7	Cleveland water freezes

	San Franciscans start thinking favorably of LA
	Green Bay Packers fans put on T-shirts
+15 / -10	You plan a vacation in Acapulco
	Cat insists on sleeping in your bed with you
	Thunder Bayites go swimming
+10 / -12	Politicians begin to talk about the homeless
	Too cold to snow
	You need jumper cables to get the car going
0 / -18	New York landlords turn on the heat
	Sheboygan brats grilled on the patio, yum!
-5 / -21	You can hear your breath
	You plan a vacation in Hawaii
-10 / -23	American cars don't start
	Too cold to skate
-15 / -26	You can cut your breath and use it to build an igloo
	Miamians cease to exist
	Canadians lick flagpoles
-20 / -29	Cat insists on sleeping in your pajamas with you
	Politicians actually do something about the homeless
	People in LaCrosse think about taking down screens
-25 / -32	Too cold to kiss
	You need jumper cables to get the driver going
	Japanese cars don't start
	Milwaukee Brewers head for spring training
-30 / -34	You plan a two-week hot bath
	Pilsner freezes
	Bock beer production begins
	Thunder Bayites shovel snow off roof
-38 / -39	Mercury freezes
	Too cold to think

	Canadians button top button
-40 / -40	Californians disappear
	Car insists on sleeping in your bed with you
	Thunder Bayites put on sweaters
-50 / -46	Congressional hot air freezes
	Alaskans close the bathroom window
	Green Bay Packers practice indoors
-60 / -51	Walruses abandon Aleutians
	Sign on Mount St. Helens: "Closed for the Season"
	Thunder Bayites put gloves away, take out mittens
	Boy Scouts in Eau Claire start Klondike Derby
-70 / -57	Glaciers in Central Park
	Hudson residents replace diving boards with hockey nets
	Green Bay snowmobilers organize trans lake race to Sault Ste. Marie
-80 / -62	Polar bears abandon Baffin Island
	Rhinelander Birkebeiner
	Girl Scouts in Eau Claire start Klondike Derby
-90 / -68	Edge of Antarctica reaches Rio de Janeiro
	Lawyers chase ambulances for no more than 10 miles
	Minnesotans migrate to Wisconsin thinking it MUST be warmer
-100 / -73	Santa Claus abandons North Pole
	Canadians pull down earflaps
-173 / -114	Ethyl alcohol freezes
-297 / -183	Oxygen precipitates out of atmosphere
	Microbial life survives only on dairy products
-445 / -265	Superconductivity
-452 / -269	Helium becomes a liquid
-454 / -270	Hades freezes over
-456 / -271	Illinois drivers drop below 85 MPH on I-90

18

-458 / -272	Incumbent politician renounces a campaign contribution
-460 / -273	(Absolute Zero)
	All atomic motion ceases
	Canadians allow as to how it's getting a mite nippy.

Today's Little Axioms

- He who laughs last, thinks slowest.
- A day without sunshine is like, well, night.
- On the other hand, you have different fingers.
- Change is inevitable, except from a vending machine.
- Back up my hard drive? How do I put it in reverse?
- I just got lost in thought. It was unfamiliar territory.
- When the chips are down, the buffalo is empty.
- Seen it all, done it all, can't remember most of it.
- Those who live by the sword get shot by those who don't.
- I feel like I'm diagonally parked in a parallel universe.
- He's not dead, he's electroencephalographically challenged.
- She's always late. Her ancestors arrived on the Juneflower.
- You have the right to remain silent. Anything you say will be misquoted, then used against you.
- I wonder how much deeper the ocean would be without sponges?

One Liners

- If at first you don't succeed, skydiving is not for you.
- Nothing in the known universe travels faster than a bad check.
- Vital papers will demonstrate their vitality by moving from where you left them to where you can't find them.
- Always remember to pillage BEFORE you burn.

- The trouble with doing something right the first time is that nobody appreciates how difficult it was.

- It may be that your sole purpose in life is simply to serve as warning to others.

- Ray's Law: You can't fall off the floor.

- Paranoids are people too; they have their own problems. It's easy to criticize, but if everybody hated you, you'd be paranoid too.

- If at first you don't succeed, destroy all evidence that you tried.

- A conclusion is the place where you got tired of thinking.

- Experience is something you don't get until just after you need it.

- For every action, there is an equal and opposite criticism.

- Success always occurs in private, and failure in full view.

- To steal ideas from one person is plagiarism; to steal from many is research.

- To succeed in politics, it is often necessary to rise above your principles.

- You never really learn to swear until you learn to drive.

- The sooner you fall behind, the more time you'll have to catch up.

- Plan to be spontaneous tomorrow.

Spiritual Gifts

During the French Revolution, there were three Christians who were sentenced to die by the guillotine. One Christian had the gift of faith, one had the gift of prophecy, and the other had the gift of helps.

The Christian with the gift of faith was to be executed first. He was asked if he wanted to wear a hood over his head. He declined and said he was not afraid to die. "I have faith that God will deliver me!" he shouted bravely. His head was positioned under the guillotine, with his neck on the chopping block. He looked up at the sharp blade, said a short prayer and waited confidently. The rope was pulled, but nothing happened. His executioners were amazed and, believing that this must have been an act of God, they freed the man.

The Christian with the gift of prophecy was next. His head was positioned under the guillotine blade and he too was asked if he wanted the hood. "No," he said, "I am not afraid to die. However, I predict that God will deliver me from this guillotine!" At that, the rope was pulled and again, nothing happened. Once again, the puzzled executioners assumed this must be a miracle of God, and they freed the man.

The third Christian, with the gift of helps, was next. He was brought to the guillotine and likewise asked if he wanted to wear a hood. "No," he said, "I'm just as brave as those other two guys." The executioners then positioned him face up under the guillotine and were about to pull the rope when the man stopped them. "Hey wait a minute," he said. "I think I just found the problem with your guillotine."

Dead Politicians

A bus of politicians is driving by a farm where a man lives alone. The bus driver, caught up in the beautiful scenery, loses control and crashes into the ditch. The man comes out and finding the politicians, buries them.

The next day, the police are at the farm questioning the man. "So you buried all the politicians?" asked the police officer. "Were they all dead?"

The man answered, "Some said they weren't, but you know how politicians lie."

The Head Hog

The church secretary picked up the phone and heard a very "countryfied" voice on the other end saying, "I want to talk to the head hog at the trough!"

Puzzled, the secretary said, "Excuse me sir?"

He repeated, "I want to talk to the head hog at the trough!"

She then realized the man wanted to talk to the pastor. Somewhat indignant she said, "Sir, if you want to talk to our pastor, you will have to address him properly. You should call him Pastor, or Reverend, or Brother, but you certainly cannot refer to him as the Head Hog at the Trough!"

The man on the other end said in a country drawl, "Oh, I just wanted to donate $10,000 to the church."

The secretary promptly replied, "Can you hold please, I think the big pig just walked through the door!"

Things Dogs Must Try To Remember

- The garbage collector is NOT stealing our stuff even though I haven't had a chance to rip the bag to shreds to see what was in it.

- I do not need to suddenly stand straight up when I'm lying under the coffee table.

- I will not roll my toys behind the fridge.

- I must shake the rainwater out of my fur BEFORE entering the house.

- I will not eat the cats' food, before or after they eat it.

- I will stop trying to find the few remaining pieces of clean carpet in the house when I am about to throw up or have an accident.

- I will not throw up in the car.

- I will not roll on dead seagulls, fish, crabs, etc.

- I will not chew my human's toothbrush and not tell them.

- I will not chew crayons or pens, especially not the red ones, or my people will think I am hemorrhaging.

- I will not take whatever I please and hide it under the bed so my people can have a scavenger hunt looking for it.

- When in the car, I will not insist on having the window rolled down when it's raining outside.

- The sofa is not a face towel. Neither are Mom and Dad's laps.

- My head does not belong in the refrigerator.

- I will not bite the officer's hand when he reaches in for Mom's driver's license and car registration.

- I will not stand around Mom when she is cooking or when she is carrying her coffee, so she won't trip over me.

- I will not beg for food at the supper table, and especially not eat someone's food if they leave it for just a moment.

- I will not tear up the patio furniture, or put holes in the screen so I may jump in and lounge, just because I don't want to stay outside for more than 2 minutes.

- I will not chase the cat, and knock over breakable things in the process.

- We don't have a doorbell. I will not bark each time I hear one on TV.

Somebody is Knocking

A new pastor moved into town and went out one Saturday to visit his parishioners. All went well until he came to one house. It was obvious that someone was home, but no one came to the door even after he had knocked several times.

Finally, he took out his card, wrote on the back "Revelation 3:20 " and stuck it in the door.

The next day, as he was counting the offering he found his card in the collection plate. Below his message was the notation "Genesis 3:10".

Revelation 3:20 reads:

"Behold, I stand at the door and knock. If any man hear my voice, and opens the door, I will come in to him, and will dine with him, and he will with me."

Genesis 3:10 reads:

"And he said, I heard thy voice in the garden, and I was afraid, because I was naked."

Somebody is at the Door

A priest is walking down the street one day when he notices a very small boy trying to press a doorbell on a house across the street. However, the boy is very small and the doorbell is too high for him to reach.

After watching the boy's efforts for some time, the priest moves closer to the boy's position. He steps smartly across the street, walks up behind the little fellow and, placing his hand kindly on the child's shoulder leans over and gives the doorbell a solid ring.

Crouching down to the child's level, the priest smiles benevolently and asks, "And now what, my little man?"

The boy replies, "Now we run!"

Bunch of Puns

- Two Eskimos sitting in a kayak were chilly, but when they lit a fire in the craft it sank - proving once and for all that you can't have your kayak and heat it too.

- Two boll weevils grew up in South Carolina. One went to Hollywood and became a famous actor. The other stayed behind in the cotton fields and never amounted to much. The second one, naturally, became known as the lesser of two weevils.

- A three-legged dog walks into a saloon in the Old West. He sidles up to the bar and announces: "I'm looking for the man who shot my paw."

- A neutron goes into a bar and asks the bartender, "How much for a beer?" The bartender replies, "For you, no charge."

- Two atoms are walking down the street and they run into each other. One says to the other, "Are you all right?" "No, I lost an electron!" "Are you sure?" "Yeah, I'm positive!"

- Did you hear about the Buddhist who refused his dentist's Novocain during root canal work? He wanted to transcend dental medication.

- A group of chess enthusiasts checked into a hotel and were standing in the lobby discussing their recent tournament victories. After about an hour, the manager came out of the office and asked them to disperse. "But why? " they asked as they moved off. "Because," he said, "I can't stand chess nuts boasting in an open foyer."

- A woman has twins, and gives them up for adoption. One of them goes to a family in Egypt and is named "Amal." The other goes to a family in Spain; they name him "Juan." Years later, Juan sends a picture of himself to his mom. Upon receiving the picture, she tells her husband that she wishes she also had a picture of Amal. Her husband responds, "But they are twins - if you've seen Juan, you've seen Amal."

- This guy goes into a restaurant for a Christmas breakfast while in his hometown for the holidays. After looking over the menu he says, "I'll just have the eggs Benedict." His order comes a while later and it's served on a big, shiny hubcap. He asks the waiter, "What's with the hubcap?" The waiter sings, "O, there's no plate like chrome for the hollandaise!"

- A doctor made it his regular habit to stop at a bar for a hazelnut daiquiri on his way home. The bartender knew of his habit, and would always have the drink waiting at precisely 5:03 p.m. One afternoon, as the end of the workday approached, the bartender was dismayed to find that he was out of hazelnut extract. Thinking quickly, he threw together a daiquiri made with hickory nuts and set it on the bar. The doctor came in took one sip of the drink and exclaimed, "This isn't a hazelnut daiquiri!"

"No, I'm sorry," replied the bartender. "It's a hickory daiquiri, doc."

- A hungry lion was roaming through the jungle looking for something to eat. He came across two men. One was sitting under a tree reading a book; the other was typing away on his typewriter. The lion quickly pounced on the man reading the book and devoured him. Even the king of the jungle knows that readers digest and writers cramp.

- There was a man who entered a local paper's pun contest. He sent in ten different puns, in the hope that at least one of the puns would win. Unfortunately, no pun in ten did.

Five Things You Do Not Want to Hear When Calling Tech Support

1. "Duuuuuude! Bummer!"

2. "In layman's term, we call that the 'Hindenburg Effect.'"

3. "Your problem can be fixed, but you're going to need a butter knife, a roll of duct tape and a car battery."

4. "Press 1 for Support.
   Press 2 if you are with '60 Minutes.'
   Press 3 if you're with the FTC."

5. "Hold on a second, please ... Mom! Timmy is hitting me!!!"

Pillsbury Dough Boy Dead at 71

Veteran Pillsbury spokesman, Pop N. Fresh, died yesterday of a severe yeast infection. He was 71.

Fresh was buried in one of the largest funeral ceremonies in recent years. Dozens of celebrities turned out, including Mrs. Butterworth, the California Raisins, Hungry Jack, Betty Crocker, and the Hostess Twinkies.

The graveside was piled high with flours as long-time friend Aunt Jemima delivered the eulogy, describing Fresh as a man who "never knew how much he was kneaded."

Fresh rose quickly in show business, but his later life was filled with many turnovers. He was not considered a very smart cookie, wasting much of his dough on half-baked schemes. Still, even as a crusty old man, he was a roll model for millions.

Fresh is survived by his second wife. They have two children and one in the oven. The funeral was held at 4:50 for about 20 minutes.

"Thanks" Mom

When my three-year-old son opened the birthday gift from his grandmother, he discovered a water pistol. He squealed with delight and headed for the nearest sink. I was not so pleased. I turned to Mom and said,

"I'm surprised at you. Don't you remember how we used to drive you crazy with water guns?"

Mom smiled and then replied, "Oh, I remember...."

Country Boys

These two country boys, brothers, were knocking around one lazy summer day and thought it would be a good prank to push over the outhouse. They crept up from an advantageous direction like a couple of commandos, pushed the outhouse over on one side and headed for the woods. They circled round and returned home an hour later from a completely different direction, thus trying to divert suspicion from themselves.

Upon returning, their father approached them with switch in hand and bellowed, "Did you two push the outhouse over this afternoon?"

The older boy replied, "As learned in school, I cannot tell a lie. Yes, Father, we pushed over the outhouse this afternoon."

At this revelation, the father proceeded to flail the two boys severely and sent them to bed without supper.

In the morning, the two boys meekly approached the breakfast table and took their seats. Everything was quiet until their father finally said, "Have you two learned your lesson?"

"Sure, Dad!" said the big brother. "But, in school we learned that George Washington admitted to HIS father that he'd chopped down a cherry tree and he was forgiven because he told the truth."

"Ah yes!' said the farmer. "BUT, George's DAD wasn't in the cherry tree when he chopped it down!!!"

B.O.O.K. – Introducing the
Bio-Optic Organized Knowledge software:

BOOK is a revolutionary technological breakthrough: no wires, no electric currents, no batteries. Nothing to be connected or switched on. So easy to use, even a child can operate it! Compact, portable, it can be used anywhere -- even on a beach, yards from a power point. Yet it is powerful enough to hold as much information as a CD-ROM disc! Here's how it works:

BOOK is constructed of literally hundreds of sequentially numbered sheets of paper (recyclable), each capable of holding thousands of bits of information. The pages are locked together with a custom fit device (a "binder"), which maintains each sheet in its correct sequence.

Opaque Paper Technology (OPT) allows the manufacturer to utilize BOTH sides of each sheet, thus doubling information density while cutting costs. Sheets are scanned optically, registering information directly to the brain -- the most efficient interface yet developed!

And simple: a flick of a finger takes you to the next sheet!

BOOK may be taken up at any time and used merely by opening it!

BOOK never crashes or requires rebooting. The "browse" feature permits you to move instantly to any single sheet, AND move forward and backward as you wish. Forget scrolling arrows or multiple key commands! BOOK often comes with an "index" feature that pinpoints the exact sheet location of any selected information for instant retrieval.

An optional "BOOKmark" accessory allows you to open book at THE EXACT PLACE YOU LEFT IT IN A PREVIOUS SESSION ... even if BOOK has been closed!

Best of all, BOOKmarks fit universal design standards ...any BOOKmark can be used in any BOOK by any manufacturer!

A brand new BOOKmark can even be used in a BOOK that predates it by months, even years!

Should you wish to store numerous views in a single book, multiple BOOKmarks can be used.

You also have the option to make personal notes next to BOOK text entries with an optional programming tool, Portable Erasable-Nib Cryptic Intercommunication Language Stylus (PENCILS).

Portable, durable, and affordable, BOOK is being hailed as the precursor of a new information-delivery wave. BOOK's appeal is so certain that thousands of self-employed content creators (like me) have committed to the platform, and edit technicians are evaluating their submissions.

Life is short. Information is dear. Forget the Internet. When deciding to access information, think BOOK.

Hickbonics

The Association of Southern Schools has decided to pursue some of the seemingly endless taxpayer dollar pipeline through Washington designating Southern slang, or "Hickbonics," as a language to be taught in all Southern schools. A speaker of this language would be a Hickophone. The following are excerpts from the Hickbonics/English dictionary:

HEIDI (noun) - Greeting

HIRE YEW - Complete sentence. Remainder of greeting.

>   Usage: "Heidi, Hire yew?"

BARD (verb) - Past tense of the infinitive "to borrow."

>   Usage: "My brother bard my pickup truck."

JAWJUH (noun) - The State north of Florida. Capitol is Lanner.

>   Usage: "My brother from Jawjuh bard my pickup truck."

BAMMER (noun) - The State west of Jawjuh. Capitol is Berminhayum.

>   Usage: "A tornader jes went through Bammer an' left $20,000,000 in improvements."

MUNTS (noun) - A calendar division.

>   Usage: "My brother from Jawjuh bard my pickup truck, and I ain't herd from him in munts."

THANK (verb) - Ability to cognitively process.

>   Usage: "Ah thank ah'll have a bare."

BARE (noun) - An alcoholic beverage made of barley, hops, and yeast.

>   Usage: "Ah thank ah'll have a bare."

IGNERT (adjective) - Not smart.

>   Usage: "Them bammer boys sure are ignert!"

RANCH (noun) - A tool used for tight'nin' bolts.

>   Usage: "I thank I left my ranch in the back of that pickup truck my brother from Jawjuh bard a few munts ago."

ALL (noun) - A petroleum-based lubricant.

>   Usage: "I sure hope my brother from Jawjuh puts all in my pickup truck."

FAR (noun) - A conflagration.

>   Usage: "If my brother from Jawjuh don't change the all in my pickup truck, that thing's gonna catch far."

TAR (noun) - A rubber wheel.

Usage: "Gee, I hope that brother of mine from Jawjuh don't git a flat tar in my pickup truck."

TIRE (noun) - A tall monument.

Usage: "Lord willin' and the creek don't rise, I sure do hope to see that Eiffel Tire in Paris sometime."

RETARD (verb) - To stop working.

Usage: "My grampaw retard at age 65."

FAT (noun) (verb) - A battle or combat; to engage in battle or combat.

Usage: "You younguns keep fat'n, n' ah'm gonna whup y'uh."

RATS (noun) - Entitled power or privilege.

Usage: "We Southerners are willin' to fat for are rats."

FARN (adjective) - Not domestic.

Usage: "I cuddint unnerstand a wurd he sed...must be from some farn country."

DID (adjective) - Not alive.

Usage: "He's did, Jim."

EAR (noun) - A colorless, odorless gas: Oxygen.

Usage: "He cain't breathe...give 'im some ear!"

BOB WAR (noun) - A sharp, twisted cable.

Usage: "Boy, stay away from that bob war fence."

JEW HERE (noun) (verb): a contraction.

Usage: "Jew here that my brother from Jawjuh got a job with that bob war fence cump'ny?"

HAZE: a contraction.

Usage: "Is Bubba smart?" "Nah...haze ignert. He ain't thanked but a minnit' n'is laf."

SEED (verb) - past tense of "to see".

VIEW: a contraction: (verb) (pronoun)

Usage: "I ain't never seed New York City... view?"

GUBMINT (noun) - A bureaucratic institution.

Usage: "Them gubmint boys shore is ignert."

Hymns for Professionals:

DENTIST:	Crown Him with many crowns
CONTRACTORS:	The church's one foundation
OBSTETRICIANS:	Come, labor on
GOLFERS:	There is a green hill far away
POLITICIANS:	Standing on the promises
LIBRARIANS:	Let all mortal flesh keep silence
LAWYERS:	In the hour of trial
DRY CLEANERS:	O for a faith that will not shrink
CREDIT CARD USERS:	A charge to keep have I
CENSUS TAKERS:	All people that on earth do dwell
TRAFFIC ENGINEERS:	Where cross the crowded ways of life
TAXATION OFFICERS:	We give thee but thine own

The Point System

For all of us guys out there who just can't figure it out, here it is. In the world of romance, one single rule applies: Make your wife happy. Do something she likes and you get points. Do something she dislikes and points are subtracted. You don't get any points for doing something she expects... Sorry, that's the way the game is played.

SIMPLE DUTIES:

You make the bed. +1

You make the bed, but forget to add the decorative pillows. 0

You throw the bedspread over rumpled sheets. -1

You leave the toilet seat up. -5

You replace the toilet paper roll when it's empty. 0

When the toilet paper roll is barren, you resort to Kleenex. -1

When the Kleenex runs out you shuffle slowly to the next bathroom. -2

You check out a suspicious noise at night. 0

You check out a suspicious noise and it's nothing. 0

You check out a suspicious noise and it's something. +5

You pummel it with a six iron. +10

It's her father. -10

HER BIRTHDAY:

You take her out to dinner. 0

You take her out to dinner and it's not a sports bar. +1

Okay, it is a sports bar. -2

And it's all-you-can-eat night. -3

It's a sports bar, it's all-you-can-eat night, and your face is painted the colors of your favorite team. -10

A NIGHT OUT WITH THE BOYS:

Go out with a pal. -5

And the pal is happily married. -4

Or frighteningly single. -7

And he drives a Mustang. -10

A NIGHT OUT:

You take her to a movie. +2

You take her to a movie she likes. +4

You take her to a movie you hate. +6

You take her to a movie you like. -2

It's called DeathCop 3. -3

You lied and said it was a foreign film about orphans. -15

YOUR PHYSIQUE:

You develop a noticeable potbelly. -15

You develop a noticeable potbelly and exercise to get rid of it. +10

You develop a noticeable potbelly and resort to loose jeans and baggy Hawaiian shirts. -30

You say, "I don't care because you have one too". -800

THE BIG QUESTION:

She asks, "Do I look fat?" -5

You hesitate in responding. -10

You reply, "Where?" -35

COMMUNICATION:

When she wants to talk about a problem, you listen, displaying what looks like a concerned expression. 0

When she wants to talk, you listen, for over 30 minutes. +5

You listen for more than 30 minutes without looking at the TV. +10

She realizes this is because you've fallen asleep. -20

Bribing a Pastor?
(You Get What You Pay For!)

During the wedding rehearsal, the groom approached the pastor with an unusual offer:

"Look, I'll give you $100 if you'll change the wedding vows. When you get to me and the part where I'm to promise to 'love, honor and obey,' I'd appreciate it if you'd just leave that part out." He passed the minister a $100 bill and walked away satisfied.

The big day comes, and the bride and groom exchange their vows. When it comes time for the groom's vows, the pastor looks the young man in the eye and says: "Will you promise to prostrate yourself before her, obey her every command and wish, serve her breakfast in bed every morning of your life and swear eternally before God and your lovely wife that you will not ever even look at another woman, as long as you both shall live?"

The groom gulped and looked around, and said in a tiny voice, "Yes."

The groom leaned toward the pastor and hissed, "I thought we had a deal."

The pastor put the $100 bill into his hand and whispered back, "She made me a much better offer."

Pilot Humor

Here are some actual maintenance complaints generally known as squawks or problems submitted recently by Qantas pilots to maintenance engineers. After attending to the squawks prior to the aircraft's next flight, the maintenance crews are required to log the details of action taken as a solution to the pilots squawks. The following are some recent squawks and subsequent responses by maintenance crews."

(P) is the problem logged by the pilot, and (S) marks the solution and action taken by maintenance engineers.

32

(P)	Left inside main tire almost needs replacement.
(S)	Almost replaced left inside main tire.
(P)	Test flight OK, except auto land very rough.
(S)	Auto land not installed on this aircraft.
(P)	#2 propeller seeping prop fluid.
(S)	#2 propeller seepage normal - - #1,3,4 propellers lack seepage.
(P)	Something loose in cockpit.
(S)	Something tightened in cockpit.
(P)	Evidence of leak on right main landing gear.
(S)	Evidence removed.
(P)	DME volume unbelievably loud.
(S)	Volume set to more believable level.
(P)	Dead bugs on windshield.
(S)	Live bugs on backorder.
(P)	Autopilot in altitude hold mode produces a 200-ft/minute descent.
(S)	Cannot reproduce problem on ground.
(P)	IFF inoperative.
(S)	IFF always inoperative in OFF mode.
(P)	Friction lock causes throttle levers to stick.
(S)	That's what they're there for!!
(P)	Number three engine missing.
(S)	Engine three found on right wing after brief search.
(P)	Aircraft handles funny.
(S)	Aircraft warned to straighten up, "fly right", and be serious!!
(P)	Target Radar hums.
(S)	Reprogrammed Target Radar with the words.

Technical Terms for Country Folk

Log on: making a wood stove hotter

Log off: don't add no more wood

Monitor: keeping an eye on the wood stove

Download: gettin the farwood off the truck

Mega Hertz: when yer not keerful getting the farwood

Floppy disc: whatcha git from tryin to carry too much farwood

Ram: that thar thing what splits the farwood

Hard drive: gettin home in the winter time

Prompt: whut the mail ain't in the winter time

Windows: what to shut when it's cold outside

Screen: what to shut when it's black fly season

Byte: what dem flys do

Chip: munchies fer the TV

Micro Chip: whut's in the bottom of the munchie bag

Modem: whacha did to the hay fields

Dot Matrix: Old Dan Matrix's wife

Lap Top: whar the kitty sleeps

Keyboard: whar ya hang the keys

Software: them plastic forks and knifes

Mouse: what eats the grain in the barn

Mouse Pad: hippie talk for the rat hole

Main frame: holds up the barn ruf

Port: fancy Flatlander wine

Enter: northerner talk fer "C'Mon in y'all"

Materialistic or What?

A very successful lawyer parked his brand-new Jag XK-8 in front of the office, ready to show it off to his colleagues. As he got out, a truck came along, too close to the curb, and completely tore off the driver's door of the Jag. The counselor immediately grabbed his cell phone, dialed 911, and it wasn't more than 5 minutes before a policeman pulled up.

Before the cop had a chance to ask any questions, the lawyer started screaming hysterically. His Jag, which he had just picked up the day before, was now completely ruined and would never be the same, no matter how the body shop tried to make it new again, etc., etc., etc.

After the lawyer finally wound down from his rant, the cop shook his head in disgust and disbelief. "I can't believe how materialistic you lawyers are," he said. "You are so focused on your possessions that you don't notice anything else."

"How can you say such a thing?" asked the lawyer.

The cop replied, "Didn't you know that your left arm is missing from the elbow down? It must have been torn off when the truck hit you."

"Oh No!" screamed the lawyer. "Where's my Rolex?"

Afraid to Cross

Two men stand at a river, which they are about to cross when they notice crocodiles looking at them.

"Are you afraid?" asks one to the other.

"Don't you know that God is merciful and God is good?""

"Yes I do," says the scared man. "But what if God suddenly chooses right now to be good to the crocodiles?"

How to Give Your Cat a Pill

1. Grasp cat firmly in your arms. Cradle its head on your elbow, just as if you were giving a baby a bottle. Coo confidently, "That's a nice kitty." Drop pill into its mouth.

2. Retrieve cat from top of lamp, and pill from under the sofa.

3. Follow same procedure as in 1. but hold cat's front paws down with left hand and back paws down with elbow of right arm. Poke pill into its mouth with right forefinger.

4. Retrieve cat from under the bed. Get new pill from bottle. (Resist impulse to get new cat.)

5. Again proceed as in 1. except when you have cat firmly cradled in the bottle-feeding position, sit down on edge of chair, fold your torso over cat, bring your right hand over your left elbow, open cat's mouth by lifting the upper jaw and pop pill in quickly. Since your head is down by your knees, you won't be able to see what you are doing. That's just as well.

6. Leave cat hanging on the drapes. Leave pill in your hair.

7. If you are a woman, have a good cry. If you are a man, have a good cry.

8. Now pull yourself together. Who's the boss here anyway? Retrieve cat and pill. Assuming position 1. say sternly, "Who is the boss here anyway?" Open the cat's mouth, take pill and Oooops!

9. This isn't working is it? Collapse and think. Aha! Those flashing claws are causing the chaos.

10. Crawl to linen closet. Drag back large beach towel. Spread towel on floor.

11. Retrieve cat from kitchen counter and pill from potted plant.

12. Spread cat on towel near one end with its head over long edge.

13. Flatten cat's front and back legs over its stomach. (Resist impulse to flatten cat.)

14. Roll cat in towel. Work fast; time and tabbies wait for no man or woman.

15. Resume position 1. Rotate your left hand to cat's head. Press its mouth at the jaw hinges like opening the petals on a snapdragon.

16. Drop pill into cat's mouth and poke gently. Voila! It's done.

17. Vacuum up loose fur (cats). Apply bandages to wounds (yours).

18. Take two aspirins and lie down.

Goober Pilots

Two Goobers (pilots) are trying to land an airplane. They start descending and as they touch the ground the one pilot screams to the other pilot: "Pull up, the runaway is ending..."

The second pilot swiftly gets the plane back up in the air.

They make a big turn and start descending again. The moment they touch the ground, the pilot screams again, "Get the plane up, the runaway is ending..."

The second pilot swiftly gets the plane back up in the air...They make a big turn and start descending again...This goes on again and again...

During their fourth descent the pilot says: "This is so stupid, they build this huge & expensive airport but with such a short runaway."

"I know" answers the second pilot, "but look how wide they made it...."

Actual Church Bulletin Bloopers

1. Scouts are saving aluminum cans, bottles, and other items to be recycled. The proceeds will be used to cripple children.

2. The outreach committee has enlisted 25 visitors to make calls on people who are not afflicted with any church.

3. Evening massage - 6 p.m.

36

4. The pastor would appreciate it if the ladies of the congregation would lend him their electric girdles for the pancake breakfast next Sunday morning.

5. The audience is asked to remain seated until the end of the recession.

6. Low Self-Esteem Support Group will meet Thursday from 7 to 8:30 p.m. Please use the back door.

7. Ushers will eat latecomers.

8. The third verse of Blessed Assurance will be sung without musical accomplishment.

9. For those of you who have children and don't know it, we have a nursery downstairs.

10. The Rev. Merriwether spoke briefly, much to the delight of the audience.

11. The pastor will preach his farewell message, after which the choir will sing, "Break Forth Into Joy."

12. During the absence of our pastor, we enjoyed the rare privilege of hearing a good sermon when J.F. Stubbs supplied our pulpit.

13. Next Sunday Mrs. Vinson will be soloist for the morning service. The pastor will then speak on "It's a Terrible Experience."

14. Due to the Rector's illness, Wednesday's healing services will be discontinued until further notice.

15. Stewardship Offertory: "Jesus Paid It All"

16. The music for today's service was all composed by George Friedrich Handel in celebration of the 300th anniversary of his birth.

17. Remember in prayer the many who are sick of our church and community.

18. The eighth-graders will be presenting Shakespeare's Hamlet in the church basement on Friday at 7 p.m. The congregation is invited to attend this tragedy.

19. The concert held in Fellowship Hall was a great success. Special thanks are due to the minister's daughter, who labored the whole evening at the piano, which as usual fell upon her.

20. Members were present at the church meeting held at the home of Mrs. Marsha Crutchfield last evening. Mrs. Crutchfield and Mrs. Rankin sang a duet, The Lord Knows Why.

21. A songfest was hell at the Methodist church Wednesday.

22. Today's Sermon: HOW MUCH CAN A MAN DRINK? with hymns from a full choir.

23. Hymn 43: "Great God, what do I see here?" Preacher: The Rev. Horace Blodgett. Hymn 47: "Hark! An awful voice is sounding"

24. On a church bulletin during the minister's illness: GOD IS GOOD Dr. Hargreaves is better.

More Musings

- What happens if you get scared half to death twice?

- Energizer Bunny arrested -- charged with battery.

- If you can't convince them, confuse them.

- Beat the 5 o'clock rush, leave work at noon!

- I couldn't repair your brakes, so I made your horn louder.

- How do you tell when you run out of invisible ink?

- Artificial intelligence is no match for natural stupidity.

- Everyone has a photographic memory, some just don't have film.

- If you choke a Smurf, what color does it turn?

- Smith & Wesson -- the original point and click interface.

- Radioactive cats have 18 half-lives.

- Who is General Failure, and why is he reading my hard disk?

- Corduroy pillows -- they're making headlines!

- All those who believe in psycho kinesis, raise my hand.

- Polynesia -- memory loss in parrots.

- Oh Lord give me patience, and give it to me NOW!

- Laughing stock -- cattle with a sense of humor.

- Why do psychics have to ask you for your name?

- Wear short sleeves! Support your right to bare arms!

- For Sale: Parachute. Only used once, never opened, small stain.

Comments Never Heard At Church

1. Hey! It's my turn to sit in the front pew.

2. I was so enthralled; I never noticed your sermon went 25 minutes over time.

3. Personally I find witnessing much more enjoyable than golf.

4. I've decided to give our church the $500 a month I used to send to TV evangelists.

5. I volunteer to be the permanent teacher for the Junior High Sunday School class.

6. Forget the denominational minimum salary; let's pay our pastor so he can live like we do.

7. I love it when we sing hymns I've never heard before!

8. Since we're all here, lets start the service early.

9. Pastor, we'd like to send you to this Bible seminar in the Bahamas.

10. Nothing inspires me and strengthens my commitment like our annual stewardship campaign.

Goober Mechanic

When my husband and I arrived at an automobile dealership to pick up our car, we were told that the keys had been accidentally locked in it. We went to the service department and found a mechanic working feverishly to unlock the driver's side door.

As I watched from the passenger's side, I instinctively tried the door handle and discovered it was open.

"Hey!" I announced to the technician. "It's open!"

"I know," answered the young man. "I already got that side."

Sleeping at Work

Just in case your boss catches you asleep at your desk, be ready to blurt out one of these excuses.

*   They told me at the blood bank that this might happen.

*   This is just a 15-minute power nap like they raved about in that time management course you sent me to.

- I was working smarter - not harder.

- Whew! I must have left the top off the whiteout.

- I wasn't sleeping! I was meditating on the mission statement and envisioning a new paradigm!

- This is one of the seven habits of highly effective people!

- I was testing the keyboard for drool resistance.

- I'm in the management training program.

- I'm actually doing a Stress Level Elimination Exercise Plan.(SLEEP) I learned at the last mandatory seminar you made me attend.

- This is in exchange for the six hours last night when I dreamed about work!

- Darn! Why did you interrupt me? I had almost figured out a solution to our biggest problem.

- The coffee machine is broken....

- Someone must have put decaf in the wrong pot.

- Boy, that cold medicine I took last night just won't wear off.

- I wasn't sleeping. I was trying to pick up my contact lens without my hands.

- The mail courier flipped out and pulled a gun so I was playing dead to avoid getting shot.

Actual Signs

Bucharest Hotel Lobby

"The lift is being fixed for the next day. During that time you will be unbearable."

Leipzig elevator

"Do not enter the lift backwards and only when lit up"

Belgrade elevator

"To move the cabin, push forward for wishing floor. If the cabin should enter more persons, each one should press a number for a wishing floor. Driving is then going alphabetically by national order"

40

Paris elevator

"Please leave your values at the front desk."

Athenian hotel

"Visitors are expected to complain at the office between the hours of....."

Moscow Hotel

"You are invited to visit the cemetery where famous Soviet composers, authors and artists are buried daily except Thursday."

Austrian ski hotel

"Do not perambulate the corridors in the hours of repose in the boots of ascension."

Swiss menu

"Our wines leave you nothing to hope for."

Polish menu

"Salad of firm's own make: limpid red beet soup with cheesy dumplings in the form of a finger; roasted duck let loose; beef rashers beaten up in the country people's fashion."

Hong Kong dress shop

"Ladies have fits upstairs."

Rhodes tailor shop

"Order your summer suit because it is big rush we will execute customers in strict rotation."

Germany's Black Forest

"It is strictly forbidden on our Black Forest camping site that people of different sex, for instance, men and women, live together in one tent unless they are married together for that reason."

Swedish furrier

"Fur coats made for ladies from their own skin."

Japanese detour sign

"Stop: Drive sideways."

Swiss mountain inn

"Special today - no ice cream."

Copenhagen airline office

"We take your bags and send them in all directions."

Budapest zoo

"Please do not feed the animals. If you have suitable food, give it to the guard on duty."

Acapulco hotel

"The manager has personally passed all the water served here."

Japanese air conditioner

"Cooles and Heates: If you want just condition of warm in your room, please control yourself."

Tokyo car rental firm

"When passenger of foot heave in sight, tootle the horn. Trumpet him melodiously at first, but if he still obstacles your passage, then tootle him with vigor."

Norwegian cocktail bar

"Ladies are requested not to have children in the bar."

Shakey's Cure

Shakey went to a psychiatrist. "Doc," he said, "I've got trouble. Every time I get into bed, I think there's somebody under it. I get under the bed, I think there's somebody on top of it. Top, under, top, under. . . you gotta help me, I'm going crazy!"

"Just put yourself in my hands for two years," said the shrink. "Come to me three times a week, and I'll cure your fears."

"How much do you charge?"

"A hundred dollars per visit."

"I'll sleep on it," said Shakey.

Six months later the doctor met Shakey on the street. "Why didn't you ever come to see me again?" asked the psychiatrist.

"For a hundred bucks a visit? A bartender cured me for ten dollars."

"Is that so! How?"

"He told me to cut the legs off the bed!"

Stork Reunion

A man took his little boy to the zoo for the very first time. Each time they would see a new animal the little boy would ask, "What's that?" Each time the father would explain. When they came to a pen with a very large bird inside the father said, "And that, Timmy, is a stork."

The boy stood there for a few moments and then began to wave and say, "Hi! I'm Timmy!" After several times of repeating this he finally turned to his father and exclaimed, "Guess I'm all grown up, Dad, he doesn't recognize me."

Battle of the Dogs

The Americans and Russians at the height of the arms race realized that if they continued in the usual manner they were going to blow up the whole world. One day they sat down and decided to settle the whole dispute with one dogfight. They would have five years to breed the best fighting dog in the world and then whichever side's dog won, they would be entitled to dominate the world.

The Russians found the biggest meanest Doberman and Rottweiler female dogs in the world and bred them with the biggest meanest Siberian wolves. They selected only the biggest and strongest puppy from each litter, and removed his siblings, which gave him all the milk. After five years they came up with the biggest, meanest dog the world had ever seen.

Its cage needed steel bars that were five inches thick and nobody could get near it.

When the day came for the dogfight, the Americans showed up with a strange animal. It was a nine foot long Dachshund. Everyone felt sorry for the Americans because they knew there was no way that this dog could possibly last ten seconds with the Russian dog.

When the cages were opened up, the Dachshund came out of it's cage and slowly waddled over towards the Russian dog. The Russian dog snarled and leaped out of its cage and charged the American dachshund. But, when it got close enough to bite the Dachshund's neck, the Dachshund opened its mouth and consumed the Russian dog in one bite.

There was nothing left at all of the Russian dog.

The Russians came up to the Americans shaking their heads in disbelief. "We don't understand how this could have happened. We had our best people working for five years with the meanest

Doberman and Rottweiler female dogs in the world and the biggest, meanest Siberian wolves."

"That's nothing", an American replied. "We had our best plastic surgeons working for five years to make an alligator look like a Dachshund."

More Cute Kids

On vacation with her family in Montana, a mother drove her van past a church in a small town and pointing to it, told the children that it was St. Francis' Church.

"It must be a franchise," her eight-year-old son said. "We've got one of those in our town too."

A Sunday school teacher challenged her children to take some time on Sunday afternoon to write a letter to God. They were to bring back their letter the following Sunday.

One little boy wrote: "Dear God, We had a good time at church today. Wish You could have been there."

Bouncing out of her first day in nursery school at Mount Moriah Presbyterian Church in Port Henry, New York, a three-year-old girl gleefully informed her mother: "We had juice and Billy Graham crackers!"

Rev. David A. Stammerjohn, pastor of Laboratory Presbyterian Church, Washington, Pennsylvania, spent a week at the Synod school with his two children. The school's theme focused on Moses and the Exodus.

When they returned home, his five-year-old daughter excitedly greeted her mother: "Guess what, Mommy. We made unleaded bread!"

The old pastor made it a practice to visit the parish school one day a week. He walked into the 4th grade class, where the children were studying the states, and asked them how many states they could name.

They came up with about 40 names. He jokingly told them that in his day students knew the names of all the states.

One lad raised his hand and said, "Yes, but in those days there were only 13."

Four-year-old Tucker Jones attended the vacation Bible school at our church. The theme was "Discipleship and Saving Mother Earth." His mother, Trish Jones, asked Tucker what he had learned.

He immediately told her all about "Jesus and the 12 recycles."

Dishonesty Doesn't Pay

One year, at Western University, there were these two guys who were taking Chemistry and who did pretty well on all of the quizzes and the midterms and labs, etc., such that going into the final they had a solid A.

These two friends were so confident going into the final that the weekend before finals week (even though the Chem final was Monday morning), they decided to go over to Toronto and party with some friends there during the Vanier Cup weekend. So they did this and had a great time.

However, with their partying and everything, they overslept all day Sunday and didn't make it back to Western until early Monday morning. Rather than taking the final then, what they did was to find their Professor after the final and explain to him why they missed the final. They told him that they went to Toronto for the weekend, and had planned to come back in time to study, but that they had a flat tire on the way back and didn't have a spare and couldn't get help for a long time and so were late getting back to campus.

The Professor thought this over and then agreed that they could make up the final on the following day. The two guys were elated and relieved. So, they studied that night and went in the next day at the time the Prof had told them. He placed them in separate rooms and handed each of them a test booklet and told them to begin. They looked at the first problem, which was something simple about morality and solutions and was worth 5 points.

"Cool" they thought, "this is going to be easy." They did that problem and then turned the page. They were unprepared, however, for what they saw on the next page.

It said: (95 points) Which tire?

Diaper Change

"Here's your problem," says the doctor to the first-time father.

"This baby's in serious need of a diaper change."

Looking baffled, the man replies, "But the package says it's good for 8 to 10 pounds!"

Sunday Drive

Sitting on the side of the highway waiting to catch speeding drivers, a State Police Officer sees a car puttering along at 22 MPH. He thinks to himself, "This driver is just as dangerous as a speeder!" So he turns on his lights and pulls the driver over.

Approaching the car, he notices that there are five elderly ladies, two in the front seat and three in the back, wide-eyed and white as ghosts. The driver, obviously confused, says to him, "Officer, I don't understand. I was doing exactly the speed limit! What seems to be the problem?"

"Ma'am," the officer replies, "you weren't speeding, but you should know that driving slower than the speed limit can also be a danger to other drivers."

"Slower than the speed limit? No sir, I was doing the speed limit exactly...twenty-two miles an hour!" the woman says a bit proudly.

The State Police officer, trying to contain a chuckle explains to her that "22" was the route number, not the speed limit. A bit embarrassed, the woman grinned and thanked the officer for pointing out her error.

"But before I let you go, Ma'am, I have to ask... is everyone in this car OK? These women seem awfully shaken and they haven't muttered a single peep this whole time," the officer asks with concern.

"Oh, they'll be all right in a minute officer. We just got off Route 119."

Calf Birth

A man was helping one of his cows give birth, when he noticed his 4-year-old son standing wide-eyed at the fence, soaking in the whole event. The man thought, "Great, he's 4 and I'm gonna have to start explaining the birds and bees. No need to jump the gun, I'll just let him ask, and I'll answer."

After everything was over, the man walked over to his son and said, "Well son, do you have any questions?"

"Just one," gasped the still wide-eyed lad. "How fast was that calf going when he hit that cow?"

Good Guess

The Sunday school lesson for the day was about Noah's Ark, so the pre-school teacher in our Kentucky church decided to get her small pupils involved by playing a game in which they identified animals.

"I'm going to describe something to you. Let's see if you can guess what it is. First: I'm furry with a bushy tail and I like to climb trees."

The children looked at her blankly.

"I also like to eat nuts, especially acorns."

No response. This wasn't going well at all!

"I'm usually brown or gray, but sometimes I can be black or red."

Desperate, the teacher turned to a perky four-year-old who was usually good about coming up with the answers. "Michelle, what do you think?"

Michelle looked hesitantly at her classmates and replied, "Well, I know the answer has to be Jesus, but it sure sounds like a squirrel to me!"

Healthy Life

In the smoking car the conversation turned to the merits and demerits of various ways of preserving health.

One stout, florid man held forth with great eloquence on the subject. "Look at me!" he said. "Never a day's sickness in my life, and all due to simple food. Why, gentlemen," he continued, "from the age of twenty to that of forty I lived an absolutely simple regular life----no effeminate delicacies, no late hours, no extravagances.

Every day, in fact, summer and winter, I was in bed regularly at nine o'clock and up again at five in the morning. I worked from eight to one, then had dinner--a plain dinner, mark my words: after that, an hour's exercise; then--"

"Excuse me, sir," interrupted the facetious stranger in the corner, "but what were you in jail for?"

Lack of Meaningful Conversation

A farmer walked into an attorney's office wanting to file for a divorce.

The attorney asked, "May I help you?"

The farmer said, "Yea, I want to get one of those dayvorce's."

The attorney said, "Well, do you have any grounds?"

The farmer said, "Yea, I got about 140 acres."

The attorney said, "No, you don't understand, do you have a case?"

The farmer said, "No, I don't have a Case, but I have a John Deere."

The attorney said, "No you don't understand, I mean do you have a grudge?"

The farmer said, "Yea I got a grudge, that's where I park my John Deere."

The attorney said, "No sir, I mean do you have a suit?"

The farmer said, "Yes sir, I got a suit. I wear it to church on Sundays."

The exasperated attorney said, "Well sir, does your wife beat you up or anything?"

The farmer said, "No sir, we both get up about 4:30."

Finally, the attorney says, "Okay, let me put it this way. WHY DO YOU WANT A DIVORCE?"

And the farmer says, "Well, I can never have a meaningful conversation with her."

Carjacking Foiled

An elderly lady did her shopping and upon return found four males in her car. She dropped her shopping bags and drew her handgun, proceeding to scream at them at the top of her voice that she knows how to use it and that she will if required, so get out of the car.

The four men didn't wait around for a second invitation but got out and ran like mad, whereupon the lady proceeded to load her shopping bags in the back of the car and got into the drivers seat.

Small problem, her key wouldn't fit the ignition.

Her car was identical and parked four or five spaces further down. She loaded her bags into her car and drove to the police station. The sergeant that she told the story to nearly tore himself in two with laughter and pointed to the other end of the counter where 4 pale white males were reporting a car-jacking by a mad elderly white woman.

No charges were filed.

A Job Worse Than Yours

The San Francisco Zoo has an elephant named Calle who has a chronic illness, requiring medication. The zoo people couldn't get Calle to take her dose orally, so a pharmacologist developed a suppository.

The 10-inch-long, four-pound, cocoa-butter bullets are crafted by the good folks at Guittard Chocolates in Burlingame. Administering the DAILY medication takes five zoo workers, including one person to distract Calle with treats and one person who wears a full-arm glove.

So, there are at least FIVE people who have a job worse than yours!

Now stop complaining and get back to work!

2 Plus

A mathematician, a statistician and an accountant apply for the same job. The interviewer calls in the mathematician and asks, "What do two plus two equal?"

The mathematician replies, "Four."

The interviewer asks, "Four, exactly?"

The mathematician looks at the interviewer incredulously and says, "Yes, four, exactly."

Then the interviewer calls in the statistician and asks the same question, "What do two plus two equal?"

The statistician says, "On average, four - give or take ten percent, but on average, four."

Then the interviewer calls in the accountant and poses the same question, "What do two plus two equal?"

The accountant gets up, locks the door, closes the shade, sits down next to the interviewer and says, "What do you want it to equal?"

Going to Disneyworld

"Hey Grandpa! Can you make a noise like a frog?"

"I think I can do that. Why?"

"'Cuz Dad says when you croak, we're going to Disneyworld."

Stuff to Ponder

- Did you ever notice when you blow in a dog's face he gets mad at you? But when you take him in a car he sticks his head out the window.

- Have you ever noticed? Anybody going slower than you is an idiot, and anyone going faster than you is a maniac.

- You have to stay in shape. My grandmother, she started walking five miles a day when she was 60. She's 97 today and we don't know where she is.

- I'm not into working out. My philosophy: No pain, no pain.

- The reason most people play golf is to wear clothes they would not be caught dead in otherwise.

- I'm desperately trying to figure out why kamikaze pilots wore helmets.

- Anytime four New Yorkers get into a cab together without arguing, a bank robbery has just taken place.

- I voted for the Democrats because I didn't like the way the Republicans were running. Which is turning out to be like shooting yourself in the head to stop your headache.

- I have six locks on my door all in a row. When I go out, I lock every other one. I figure no matter how long somebody stands there picking the locks, they are always locking three.

- Ever wonder if illiterate people get the full effect of alphabet soup?

- I had a linguistics professor who said that it's man's ability to use language that makes him the dominant species on the planet. That may be. But I think there's one other thing that separates us from animals. We aren't afraid of vacuum cleaners.

- The statistics on sanity are that one out of every four Americans is suffering from some form of mental illness. Think of your three best friends. If they are okay, then it's you.

- Now they show you how detergents take out bloodstains, a pretty violent image there. I think if you've got a T-shirt with a bloodstain all over it, maybe laundry isn't your biggest problem. Maybe you should get rid of the body before you do the wash.

- I ask people why they have deer heads on their walls. They always say because it's such a beautiful animal. There you go. I think my mother is attractive, but I only have photographs of her.

- A lady came up to me on the street and pointed at my suede jacket. "You know a cow was murdered for that jacket"? she sneered. I replied in a psychotic tone, "I didn't know there were any witnesses. Now I'll have to kill you too."

- I always wanted to be somebody, but I should have been more specific.

Dad Lines

- I figured out why they call our language the "Mother Tongue." Fathers never get a chance to use much of it.

- Say what you will about healthy eating and all, but I've always found it awfully difficult to explain to my son (who's 6'4" to my 6' in height), why junk food is bad for you.

- One time my kids wanted to surprise me with a good breakfast in bed on Father's Day. They put a cot in the kitchen.

- If you think about it, Adam had more trouble than any of the rest of us buying his Father a gift for Father's Day. I mean, what do you get somebody who's Everything?

- I started early teaching my kids the value of a dollar. From then on, they demanded their allowances in gold.

Haiku Error Messages

Sony has announced its own computer operating system now available on its hot new portable PC called the Vaio. Instead of producing the cryptic error messages characteristic of Microsoft's Windows 95, 3.1, and DOS operating systems, Sony's chairman Asai Tawara said, "We intend to capture the high ground by putting a human, Japanese face on what has been, until now, an operating system that reflects Western cultural hegemony.

For example, we have replaced the impersonal and unhelpful Microsoft error messages with our own Japanese haiku poetry." The chairman went on to give examples of Sony's new error messages:

A file that big?	Chaos reigns within.
It might be very useful.	Reflect, repent, and reboot.
But now it is gone.	Order shall return.
- - - - - - - - - - - - - - - -	- - - - - - - - - - - - - - - - -
The Web site you seek	ABORTED effort:
cannot be located but	Close all that you have.
endless others exist	You ask way too much.
- - - - - - - - - - - - - - - -	- - - - - - - - -

Yesterday it worked
Today it is not working
Windows is like that.

- - - - - - - - - - - - - - - - - -

First snow, then silence.
This thousand dollar screen dies
so beautifully.

- - - - - - - - - - - - - - - - - -

With searching comes loss
and the presence of absence:
"My Novel" not found.

- - - - - - - - - - - - - - - - - -

Windows NT crashed.
I am the Blue Screen of Death.
No one hears your screams.

- - - - - - - - - - - - - - - - - -

Stay the patient course
Of little worth is your ire
The network is down

- - - - - - - - - - - - - - - - - -

A crash reduces
your expensive computer to
a simple stone.

- - - - - - - - - - - - - - - - - - -

Three things are certain:
Death, taxes, and lost data
Guess which has occurred.

- - - - - - - - - - - - - - - - - - -

You step in the stream,
but the water has moved on.
This page is not here.

- - - - - - - - - - - - - - - - - - -

Out of memory.
We wish to hold the whole sky,
But we never will.

- - - - - - - - - - - - - - - - - - -

Having been erased,
The document you're seeking
Must now be retyped.

- - - - - - - - - - - - - - - - - - -

The English Language

Lets face, it English is a stupid language.
There is no egg in the eggplant
And no ham in the hamburger.
And neither pine nor apple in the pineapple.
English muffins were not invented in England.
French fries were not invented in France.
We sometimes take English for granted
But if we examine its paradoxes we find that

52

Quicksand takes you down slowly,

Boxing rings are square,

And a guinea pig is neither from Guinea nor is it a pig.

If writers write, how come fingers don't fing?

If the plural of tooth is teeth

Shouldn't the plural of phone booth be phone beeth?

If the teacher taught, why didn't the preacher praught?

If a vegetarian eats vegetables what the heck does a humanitarian eat?

Why do people recite at a play yet play at a recital,

Park on driveways and drive on parkways?

How can the weather be as hot as hell on one day and as cold as hell on another?

You have to marvel at the unique lunacy

Of a language where a house can burn up as it burns down,

And in which you fill in a form by filling it out,

And a bell is only heard once it goes!

English was invented by people, not computers

And it reflects the creativity of the human race

(Which of course isn't a race at all)

That is why when the stars are out they are visible

But when the lights are out they are invisible,

And why it is that when I wind up my watch it starts

But when I wind up this poem it ends.

In a Few Moments

So far today, Lord, I've done all right. I haven't gossiped, haven't lost my temper, and haven't been greedy, grumpy, nasty, selfish or overindulgent.

I am thankful for that, Lord.

In a few moments, Lord, the alarm will ring and I am going to get out of bed. From that point on, I am probably going to need your help. Amen.

Quotes From 11 Year Olds' Science Exams

The following are all quotes from 11 year olds' science exams:

"Water is composed of two gins, Oxygin and Hydrogin. Oxygin is pure gin. Hydrogin is gin and water."

"When you breathe, you inspire. When you do not breathe, you expire."

"H20 is hot water, and CO2 is cold water."

"To collect fumes of sulphur, hold down a deacon over a flame in test tube."

"When you smell an odorless gas, it is probably carbon monoxide."

"Nitrogen is not found in Ireland because it is not found in a free state."

"Three kinds of blood vessels are arteries, vanes, and caterpillars."

"Blood flows down one leg and up the other."

"Respiration is composed of two acts, first inspiration, and then expectoration."

"The moon is a planet just like the earth, only it is even deader."

"Dew is formed on leaves when the sun shines down on them and makes them perspire."

"A super-saturated solution is one that holds more than it can hold."

"Mushrooms always grow in damp places and so they look like umbrellas."

"The body consists of three parts - the brainium, the borax and the abominable cavity. The brainium contains the brain, the borax contains the heart and lungs, and the abominable cavity contains the bowels, of which there are five - a, e, i, o and u."

"Momentum: What you give a person when they are going away."

"Planet: A body of earth surrounded by sky."

"Rhubarb: A kind of celery gone bloodshot."

"Vacuum: A large, empty space where the pope lives."

"Before giving a blood transfusion, find out if the blood is affirmative or negative."

"To remove dust from the eye, pull the eye down over the nose."

"For a nosebleed: Put the nose much lower than the body until the heart stops."

"For fainting: Rub the person's chest or, if a lady, rub her arm above the hand instead."

"For dog bite: Put the dog away for several days. If he has not recovered, then kill it."

"For asphyxiation: Apply artificial respiration until the patient is dead."

"For head cold: Use an agonizer to spray the nose until it drops in your throat."

"To keep milk from turning sour: Keep it in the cow."

"The pistol of a flower is its only protection against insects."

"The alimentary canal is located in the northern part of Indiana."

"The skeleton is what is left after the insides have been taken out and the outsides have been taken off. The purpose of the skeleton is something to hitch meat to."

"A permanent set of teeth consists of eight canines, eight cuspids, two molars, and eight cuspidors."

"The tides are a fight between the Earth and Moon. All water tends toward the moon, because there is no water in the moon, and nature abhors a vacuum. I forget where the sun joins in this fight."

"A fossil is an extinct animal. The older it is, the more extinct it is."

"Equator: A menagerie lion running around the Earth through Africa."

"Germinate: To become a naturalized German."

"Liter: A nest of young puppies."

"Magnet: Something you find crawling all over a dead cat."

The Parrot and the Magician

A magician was working on a cruise ship in the Caribbean. The audience would be different each week, so the magician allowed himself to do the same tricks over and over again.

There was only one problem: The captain's parrot saw the shows each week and began to understand how the magician did every trick. Once he understood he started shouting in the middle of the show:

"Look, it's not the same hat."

"Look, he is hiding the flowers under the table."

"Hey, why are all the cards the Ace of Spades?"

The magician was furious but couldn't do anything; it was, after all, the captain's parrot.

One day the ship had an accident and sank. The magician found himself on a piece of wood in the middle of the ocean with the parrot, of course.

They stared at each other with hate, but did not utter a word. This went on for a day and then another and another.

After a whole week the parrot said: "OK, I give up. Where's the boat?"

Drag Racing Moped

A hip young man goes out and buys the best car available: a 1997 Turbo Z123DX. It is the best and most expensive car in the world, and it runs him $500,000. He takes it out for a spin, and, while doing so, stops for a red light.

An elderly man on a moped (both looking about 90 years old) pulls up next to him. The old man looks over the sleek, shiny surface of the car and asks, "What kind of car ya' got there, sonny?"

The young many replies, "A 1997 Turbo Z123DX. They cost $500,000."

"That's a lot of money!" says the old man, shocked. "Why does it cost so much?"

"Because this car can do up to 320 miles an hour!" states the cool dude proudly.

The moped driver asks, "Can I take a look inside?"

"Sure," replies the owner.

So, the old man leans up against the car, pokes his head in the window, and looks around. Then, leaning back on his moped, the old man says, "That's a pretty nice car, all right."

Just then, the light changes, so the young man decides to show the old man what his car can do. He floors it, and within 30 seconds the speedometer reads 320 mph.

Suddenly, he notices a dot in his rear view mirror. It seems to be getting closer! He slows down a little to see what it could be, and suddenly, whhooossshhh! Something whips by him, going much faster!

"What on earth could be going faster than my Turbo Z123DX?" the young man asks himself. Then, ahead of him, he sees a dot coming toward him. Whooosshh! It goes by again! And, it almost looked like the old man on the moped!

"Couldn't be," thinks the guy. "How could a moped outrun a Turbo Z123DX?"

Again, he sees a dot in his rear view mirror! Whooosh, Ka-Bbblaamm! It plows into the back of his car, demolishing the rear end.

The young man stops the car, jumps out, and it's the old man!! Of course, the moped and the old man are hurting for certain. He runs up to the moaning old man and says, "You're hurt bad! Is there anything I can do for you?"

The old man groans and replies, "Yes. Unhook my suspenders from your side-view mirror!"

Vampire Bat

A young vampire bat came flapping in from the night, covered in fresh blood and perched himself on the roof of the cave to get some sleep.

Before long, all the other bats smelled the blood and began hassling him about where he got it. He was tired and needing a rest, so he told them to please leave him alone. However, it was clear that he wasn't going to get any sleep until he satisfied their curiosity.

"OK!" he said with exasperation, "follow me," and he flew out of the cave with hundreds of bats following close behind him.

Down through the valley they went, across the river and into the deep forest. Finally he slowed down and all the other bats excitedly gathered around him.

"Do you see that tree over there?" he asked.

"Yes, yes, yes!" the bats all screamed in a frenzy.

"Good," said the first bat, "because I DIDN'T!"

You're Not a Kid Anymore When....

- You're asleep but others worry that you're dead.

- Your back goes out more than you do.

- You no longer laugh at Preparation H commercials.

- The only reason you're awake at 4 a.m. is indigestion.

- You are proud of your lawnmower.

- 8 a.m. is your idea of "sleeping in."

- People call you at 8 p.m. and ask: "Did I wake you?"

- Your high school diploma is the color of buttermilk.

- Digestion is a consideration when reading a menu.

- Nobody ever tells you to slow down.
- You make everyone be quiet during weather bulletins.
- You have a party and the neighbors don't even realize it.
- You have to get a fire permit to light your birthday candles.
- Someone breaks wind and you don't laugh.
- You're always asked to say the blessing.
- When you talk about "good grass", you're referring to someone's lawn.
- Soaking your feet in Epsom Salts borders on an erotic experience.
- Your ears are hairier than your head.
- You've seen Halley's Comet...twice.
- Your idea of the perfect nightcap is Metamucil.

Gentler Ways to Say Someone Did Something Dumb

- A few clowns short of a circus
- A few fries short of a Happy Meal
- An experiment in artificial stupidity
- Dumber than a box of hair
- A few peas short of a casserole
- Doesn't have all his Cornflakes in one box
- The wheel's spinning but the hamster's dead
- One Froot Loop shy of a full bowl
- One taco short of a combo plate
- A few feathers short of a whole duck
- All foam, no beer
- The cheese slid off the cracker
- Body by Fisher - Brains by Mattel
- Has an IQ of 2 and it takes 3 to grunt

- Warning: Objects in mirror are dumber than they appear
- Couldn't pour water out of a boot with instructions on the heel
- He fell out of the stupid tree and hit every branch on the way down
- An intellect rivaled only by garden tools
- As smart as bait
- Chimney's clogged
- Doesn't have all his dogs on one leash
- Doesn't know much but leads the league in nostril hair
- Elevator doesn't go all the way to the top floor
- Forgot to pay his brain bill
- Her sewing machine's out of thread
- His antenna doesn't pick up all the channels
- His belt doesn't go through all the loops
- If he had another brain it would be lonely
- Missing a few buttons on his remote control
- No grain in the silo
- Proof that evolution CAN go in reverse
- Receiver is off the hook
- Several nuts short of a full pouch
- Skylight leaks a little
- Slinky's kinked
- Too much yardage between the goal posts
- Surfing in Nebraska

Things My Mother Taught Me

My Mother taught me LOGIC...

> "If you fall off that swing and break your neck, you can't go to the store with me."

My Mother taught me MEDICINE...

"If you don't stop crossing your eyes, they're going to freeze that way."

My Mother taught me TO THINK AHEAD...

"If you don't pass your spelling test, you'll never get a good job!"

My Mother taught me ESP...

"Put your sweater on; don't you think that I know when you're cold?"

My Mother taught me TO MEET A CHALLENGE...

"What were you thinking? Answer me when I talk to you... Don't talk back to me!"

My Mother taught me HUMOR...

"When that lawn mower cuts off your toes, don't come running to me."

My Mother taught me how to BECOME AN ADULT...

"If you don't eat your vegetables, you'll never grow up."

My mother taught me ABOUT SEX...

"How do you think you got here?"

My mother taught me about GENETICS...

"You are just like your father!"

My mother taught me about my ROOTS...

"Do you think you were born in a barn?"

My mother taught me about the WISDOM of AGE...

"When you get to be my age, you will understand."

My mother taught me about ANTICIPATION...

"Just wait until your father gets home."

My mother taught me about RECEIVING...

"You are going to get it when we get home."

and my all time favorite thing - JUSTICE

"One day you will have kids, and I hope they turn out just like YOU . . . then you'll see what it's like."

Letters from Computer Camp

Dear Mr. Johnson:

Ann Landers wouldn't print this. I have nowhere else to turn. I have to get the word out. Warn other parents. I must be rambling on. Let me try to explain.

It's about my son, Billy. He's always been a good, normal 10 year old boy. Well, last spring we sat down after dinner to select a summer camp for Billy.

We sorted through the camp brochures. There were the usual camps with swimming, canoeing, games, singing by the campfire -- you know. There were sports camps and specialty camps for weight reduction, music, military camps and camps that specialized in Tibetan knot tying.

I tried to talk him into Camp Winnepoopoo. It's where he went last year. Billy would have none of it. Billy pulled a brochure out of his pocket. It was for a COMPUTER CAMP! We should have put our foot down right there, if only we had known. He left three weeks ago.

I DON'T KNOW WHAT HAS HAPPENED. He's changed. I can't explain it. See for yourself.

These are some of my little Billy's letters:

Letter # 1

> Dear Mom,
>
> The kids are dorky nerds. The food stinks. The computers are the only good part. We're learning how to program. Late at night is the best time to program, so they let us stay up.
>
> Love, Billy.

Letter # 2

> Dear Mom,
>
> Camp is O.K. Last night we had pizza in the middle of the night. We all get to choose what we want to drink. By the way, can you make Szechwan food? I'm getting used to it now. Gotta go, it's time for the flowchart class.
>
> Love, Billy.
>
> P.S. This is written on a word processor. Pretty swell, huh? It's spell checked too.

Letter # 3

Dear Mom,

Don't worry. We do regular camp stuff. We told ghost stories by the glow of the green computer screens. It was real neat. I don't have much of a tan 'cause we don't go outside very often. You can't see the computer screen in the sunlight anyway. That wimp camp I went to last year fed us weird food too. Lay off, Mom. I'm okay, really.

Love, Billy.

Letter # 4

Dear Mom,

I'm fine. I'm sleeping enough. I'm eating enough. This is the best camp ever. We scared the counselor with some phony worm code. It was real funny. He got mad and yelled. Can you send more money? I've got to chip in on the phone bill. Did you know that you can talk to people on a computer? Give my regards to Dad.

Love, Billy.

Letter # 5

Dear Mother,

Forget the money for the telephone. We've got a way to not pay. Sorry I haven't written. I've been learning a lot. I'm real good at getting onto any computer in the country. It's really easy! I got into the university's in less than fifteen minutes. Frederick did it in five; he's going to show me how. Frederick is my bunk partner. He's really smart. He says that I shouldn't call myself Billy anymore. So, I'm not.

Signed, William.

Letter # 6

Dear Mother,

How nice of you to come up on Parents Day. Why'd you get so upset? I haven't gained that much weight. The glasses aren't real. Everybody wears them. I was trying to fit in. Believe me, the tape on them is cool. I thought that you'd be proud of my program. After all, I've made some money on it. A publisher is sending a check for $30,000. Anyway, I've paid for the next six weeks of camp. I won't be home until late August.

Regards, William.

Letter # 7

Mother,

Stop treating me like a child. True -- physically I am only ten years old. It was silly of you to try to kidnap me. Do not try again. Remember, I can make your life miserable (i.e. - the bank, credit bureau, and government computers). I am not kidding. O.K.? I won't write again and this is your only warning. The emotions of this interpersonal communication drain me.

Sincerely, William.

What can I do, Mr. Johnson? See what I mean? It's been two weeks since I've heard from my little boy. I know that it's probably too late to save my little Billy. But, if by printing these letters you can save JUST ONE CHILD from a life of programming, please, I beg of you to do so. Thank you very much.

Sally Gates,

Concerned Parent

Employee Reviews

- "Some drink from the fountain of knowledge; he only gargled."

- "She sets low personal standards and then consistently fails to achieve them."

- "This person had delusions of adequacy."

- "Since my last report, he has reached rock bottom and has started to dig."

- "His men would follow him anywhere, but only out of morbid curiosity."

- "I would not allow this employee to breed."

- "This employee is really not so much of a has-been, but more of a definite won't be."

- "Works well when under constant supervision and cornered like a rat in a trap."

- "When she opens her mouth, it seems that this is only to change whichever foot was previously in there."

- "This employee should go far - and the sooner he starts, the better."

- "This employee is depriving a village somewhere of an idiot."

- "Got into the gene pool while the lifeguard wasn't watching."

- "A room temperature IQ."

- "A gross ignoramus -- 144 times worse than an ordinary ignoramus."

- "A prime candidate for natural deselection."

- "One-cell organisms outscore him in IQ tests."

- "Fell out of the family tree."

- "Gates are down, the lights are flashing, but the train isn't coming."

- "Has two brains; one is lost and the other is out looking for it."

- "He's so dense, light bends around him."

- "If brains were taxed, he'd get a rebate."

- "If he were any more stupid, he'd have to be watered twice a week."

- "If you stand close enough to him, you can hear the ocean."

- "One neuron short of a synapse."

Gift Parrot

There was a man who traveled all around the world.

Every city he stopped in he would buy something for his mother and send it to her. On one such stop he found a parrot that spoke thirty different languages. He immediately bought it and sent it home to his mother.

A few days later he called his mother. "Did you like the parrot?" he asked her.

"Oh yes," she replied. "It was delicious."

"WHAT!" the man cried. "You ate it!? That parrot wasn't for you to eat! It spoke thirty languages!"

The mother paused for a moment and then said, "So why didn't he say something?"

Things Moms Would Probably Never Say

- "How on earth can you see the TV sitting so far back?"

- "Yeah, I used to skip school a lot, too."

- "Just leave all the lights on . . . it makes the house look more cheery."

- "Let me smell that shirt. Yeah, it's good for another week."

- "Go ahead and keep that stray dog, honey. I'll be glad to feed and walk him every day."

- "Well, if Timmy's mom says it's okay, that's good enough for me."

- "The curfew is just a general time to shoot for. It's not like I'm running a prison around here."

- "I don't have a tissue with me . . . just use your sleeve."

- "Don't bother wearing a jacket. The wind chill is bound to improve."

Anthill Golfing

Once there was a golfer whose drive landed on an anthill.

Rather than move the ball, he decided to hit it where it lay. He gave a mighty swing. Clouds of dirt and sand and ants exploded from the spot. Everything but the golf ball. It sat in the same spot.

So he lined up and tried another shot. Clouds of dirt and sand and ants went flying again. The golf ball didn't even wiggle.

Two ants survived. One dazed ant said to the other, "Whoa! What are we going to do?"

Said the other ant: " I don't know about you, but I'm going to get on the ball."

Bungee Jumper

Two entrepreneurs, Jack and John, decided to start a bungee-jumping business south of the border. They went to Casa del Sol, Mexico, built a huge platform, and opened for business. By noon the first day, they both noticed that while everyone was watching, no one was buying tickets.

65

Jack told John to go up and jump, so everyone could see how much fun it was, and then they would buy tickets and try it.

John jumped, almost reached the ground, and sprang back up. Jack saw that his shirt was torn and his hair was mussed. John came down again and sprang back up. This time he had several bruises and his clothes were ripped to shreds. The third time down and back up, he had several open wounds, a broken arm, and was bruised over most of his body.

Jack quickly raised John to the platform and asked him what in the world was going on.

John replied, "I'm not sure. Do you know what 'pinata' means?"

Lazy Cobbler

A man went into a shoe repair store in his hometown that he had not been in for almost twenty years. He found everything just the way he remembered it. He went up to the counter and asked the man about a pair of shoes that he had left there for heel repair almost 20 years ago.

"One minute. I'll check," replied the man.

A few minutes later, the repairman came back.

"Well...?" asked the man.

"They'll be ready Tuesday."

Things You do Not Want to Hear in Surgery

- Better save that. We'll need it for the autopsy.

- Somebody call the janitor - we're going to need a mop.

- Accept this sacrifice, O Great Lord of Darkness.

- Sparky! Come back with that! Bad Dog!

- Wait a minute...if this is his spleen, then what's that?

- Hand me that...uh...that uh...thingy.

- Oh no! I just lost my Rolex.

- Oops! Hey, has anyone ever survived a full hypo of this stuff before?

- Everybody stand back! I lost my contact lens!

- Could you stop that thing from beating; it's throwing my concentration off.

- What's this doing here?

- I hate it when they're missing stuff in here.

- That's cool! Now can you make his leg twitch?!

- I wish I hadn't forgotten my glasses.

- Well folks, this will be an experiment for all of us.

- Sterile, schmerile. The floor's clean, right?

- Anyone see where I left that scalpel?

- Next, we remove the subject's brain and place it in the body of the ape.

- Now take a picture from this angle. This is truly a freak of nature.

- This patient has already had some kids, am I correct?

- Nurse, did this patient sign the organ donation card?

- Don't worry. I think it is sharp enough.

- What do you mean 'You want a divorce'!

- She's gonna blow! Everyone take cover!!!

- FIRE! FIRE! Everybody get out!

- 'And next week, we'll be learning how to stitch up a patient...'

Honest Mechanic

I was worried that my mechanic might try to rip me off, so I was relieved when he told me all I needed was blinker fluid.

Children Under Ten

Mark Twain's contention was that the most interesting information comes from children, for they tell all they know and then stop. These words of wisdom were all spoken by children under 10:

- You can listen to thunder after lightening to tell how close you came to getting hit. If you don't hear it, never mind.

- Rainbows are just to look at, not to really understand.

- South America has cold summers and hot winters, but somehow they still manage.

- Many dead animals in the past changed to fossils while others preferred to be oil.

- Genetics explains why you look like your father ... and if you don't, why you should.

- Vacuums are nothing. I only mention them to let them know we know they are there.

- Some people can tell the time by looking at the sun, but I have never been able to make out the numbers.

- We say the cause of perfume disappearing is evaporation. Evaporation gets blamed for a lot of things people forget to put the top on.

- I am not sure how clouds get formed but the clouds know how to do it and that is the important thing.

If Only Life Could Be Like A Computer!

If you messed up your life, you could press "Ctrl, Alt, Delete" and start all over!

To get your daily exercise, just click on "run"!

If you needed a break from life, click on "suspend". Hit "any key" to continue life when ready.

To get even with the neighbors, turn up the sound blaster.

To add/remove someone in your life, click settings and control panel.

To improve your appearance, just adjust the display settings.

If life gets too noisy, turn off the speakers.

When you lose your car keys, click on find.

"Help" with the chores is just a click away.

Auto insurance wouldn't be necessary. You would use your diskette to recover from a crash.

And, we could click on "SEND NOW" and a Pizza would be on its way to YOU...

Van Gogh Family Tree

After much careful research it has been discovered that the artist Vincent Van Gogh had many relatives. Among them were:

His obnoxious brother	Please Gogh
His dizzy aunt	Verti Gogh
The brother who ate prunes	Gotta Gogh
The brother who worked at a convenience store	Stopn Gogh
The brother who bleached his clothes white	Hue Gogh
The cousin from Illinois	Chica Gogh
His magician uncle	Wherediddy Gogh
His Mexican cousin	Amee Gogh
The Mexican cousin's American half-brother	Grin Gogh
The nephew who drove a stage coach	Wellsfar Gogh
The ballroom dancing aunt	Tan Gogh
The bird lover uncle	Flamin Gogh
His nephew psychoanalyst	E Gogh
The fruit loving cousin	Man Gogh
An aunt who taught positive thinking	Wayto Gogh
The little nephew	Poe Gogh
A sister who loved disco	Ahgo Gogh
And his niece who travels the country in a van	Winnie B. Gogh

Farmer's Mule

Zack and his mule were walking down the road when one of Zack's friends drove up and offered him a ride to town. Zack got into the truck while his mule ran along behind. The mule was right in back of them as they reached 55, and stayed with them as they sped up to 70.

"I'm worried about your mule," said the driver. "His tongue's hanging out."

"Which way?" asked Zack.

"Left," his friend said.

"Well, stay in this lane - he's about to pass."

One Liners

- Well, this day was a total waste of make-up.

- Make yourself at home! Clean my kitchen.

- Who are these kids and why are they calling me Mom?

- Don't bother me. I'm living happily ever after.

- I started out with nothing & still have most of it left.

- I pretend to work. They pretend to pay me.

- If I throw a stick, will you leave?

- You! Off my planet!

- Therapy is expensive; poppin' bubble wrap is cheap! You choose.

- Practice random acts of intelligence & senseless acts of self-control.

- Bottomless pit of needs & wants.

- Friendly checkout clerk. Thanks for keeping me that way!

- If I want to hear the pitter-patter of little feet, I'll put shoes on my cat.

- Does your train of thought have a caboose?

- Errors have been made. Others will be blamed.

- And your crybaby whiny opinion would be...?

- I'm not crazy; I've just been in a very bad mood for 30 years.

- If only you'd use your powers for good instead of evil...

- See no evil, hear no evil, date no evil.

- A PBS mind in an MTV world.

- Allow me to introduce my selves.

- Sarcasm is just one more service we offer.

- Whisper my favorite words: "I'll buy it for you."

- Better living through denial.

- Whatever kind of look you were going for, you missed.

- Suburbia: where they tear out the trees & then name streets after them.

- Adult child of alien invaders.

- I'm just working here till a good fast-food job opens up.

- I'm trying to imagine you with a personality.

- A cubicle is just a padded cell without a door.

- Stress is when you wake up screaming & you realize you haven't fallen asleep yet.

- Here I am! Now what are your other two wishes?

- I can't remember if I'm the good twin or the evil one.

- Don't worry. I forgot your name, too!

- Adults are just kids who owe money.

- I work 40 hours a week to be this poor.

- Can I trade this job for what's behind door #2?

- Nice perfume. Must you marinate in it?

- Too many freaks, not enough circuses.

- Chaos, panic, & disorder - my work here is done.

- Ambivalent? Well, yes and no.

- Is it time for your medication or mine?

- I plead contemporary insanity.

- And which dwarf are you?

- I refuse to star in your psychodrama.

- I thought I wanted a career; turns out I just wanted paychecks.

- How do I set a laser printer to stun?

- Meandering to a different drummer.

- I'm not tense, just terribly, terribly alert.

If You Don't Go, I Go

A church had a man in the choir who couldn't sing. Several people hinted to him that he could serve in other places, but he continued to come to the choir. The choir director became desperate and went to the pastor.

"You've got to get that man out of the choir," he said. "If you don't, I'm going to resign. The choir members are going to quit too. Please do something."

So the pastor went to the man and suggested, "Perhaps you should leave the choir."

"Why should I get out of the choir?" he asked.

"Well, five or six people have told me you can't sing."

That's nothing," the man snorted. "Fifty people have told me that you can't preach!"

Scout's Letter Home

Dear Mom,

Our scoutmaster told us all write to our parents in case you saw the flood on TV and worried. We are OK. Only 2 of our tents and 4 sleeping bags got washed away. Luckily, none of us got drowned because we were all up on the mountain looking for Jeff when it happened. Oh yes, please call Jeff's mother and tell her he is OK. He can't write because of the cast. I got to ride in one of the search & rescue jeeps. It was neat.

We never would have found him in the dark if it hadn't been for the lightning. Scoutmaster Webb got mad at Hector for going on a hike alone without telling anyone. Hector said he did tell him, but it was during the fire so he probably didn't hear him. Did you know that if you put gas on a fire, the gas can will blow up? The wet wood still didn't burn, but one of our tents did. Also some of our clothes. Larry is going to look weird until his hair grows back.

We will be home on Saturday if Scoutmaster Webb gets the car fixed. It wasn't his fault about the wreck. The brakes worked OK when we left. Scoutmaster Webb said that with a car that old you have to expect something to break down; that's probably why he can't get insurance on it. We think it's a neat car. He doesn't care if we get it dirty, and if it's hot, sometimes he lets us ride on the tailgate. It gets pretty hot with 10 people in a car.

He let us take turns riding in the trailer until the highway patrolman stopped and talked to us. Scoutmaster

Webb is a neat guy. Don't worry, he is a good driver. In fact, he is teaching brother Doug how to drive. But he only lets him drive on the mountain roads where there isn't any traffic. All we ever see up there are logging trucks.

This morning all of the guys were diving off the rocks and swimming out in the lake. Scoutmaster Webb wouldn't let me because I can't swim and Jeff was afraid he would sink because of his cast, so he let us take the canoe across the lake. It was great. You can still see some of the trees under the water from the flood. Scoutmaster Webb isn't crabby like some scoutmasters. He didn't even get mad about the life jackets. He has to spend a lot of time working on the car so we are trying not to cause him any trouble.

Guess what? We have all passed our first aid merit badges. When Rob dove in the lake and cut his arm, we got to see how a tourniquet works. Also Bruce and I threw up. Scoutmaster Webb said it probably was just food poisoning from the leftover chicken. He said they got sick that way with the food they ate in prison. I'm so glad he got out and become our scoutmaster. He said he sure figured out how to get things done better while he was doing his time.

I have to go now. We are going into town to mail our letters and buy bullets.

Don't worry about anything. We are fine.

Love, Dave

Died in the Service

One Sunday morning, the pastor noticed little Alex was staring up at the large plaque that hung in the foyer of the church.

The seven-year-old had been staring at the plaque for some time, so the pastor walked up, stood beside the boy, and said quietly, "Good morning Alex."

"Good morning pastor," replied the young man, focused on the plaque. "Pastor McGhee, what is this?" Alex asked.

"Well son, these are all the people who have died in the service," replied the pastor.

Soberly, they stood together, staring at the large plaque.

Little Alex's voice barely broke the silence when he asked quietly, "Which one, the 9:00 or the 10:30 service?"

Three Lawyers and Three Engineers

Three lawyers and three engineers are traveling by train to a conference. At the station, the three lawyers each buy tickets and watch as the three engineers buy only a single ticket.

"How are three people going to travel on only one ticket?" asked one of the three lawyers. "Watch and you'll see," answers one of the engineers.

They all board the train. The lawyers take their respective seats but all three engineers cram into a restroom and close the door behind them.

Shortly after the train has departed, the conductor comes around collecting tickets. He knocks on the restroom door and says, "Ticket, please." The door opens just a crack and a single arm emerges with a ticket in hand. The conductor takes it and moves on. The lawyers saw this and agreed it was quite a clever idea.

So after the conference, the lawyers decide to copy the engineers on the return trip and save some money. When they get to the station, they buy a single ticket for the return trip. To their astonishment, the engineers don't buy a ticket at all.

"How are you going to travel without a ticket," asks one perplexed lawyer. "Watch and you'll see," says one of the engineers.

When they board the train the three lawyers cram into a restroom and the three engineers cram into another one nearby. The train departs. Shortly afterward, one of the engineers leaves his restroom and walks over to the restroom where the lawyers are hiding. He knocks on the door and says, "Ticket, please."

Funny Signs in England...

- AUTOMATIC WASHING MACHINES: PLEASE REMOVE ALL YOUR CLOTHES WHEN THE LIGHT GOES OUT

- BARGAIN BASEMENT UPSTAIRS

- WOULD THE PERSON WHO TOOK THE STEP LADDER YESTERDAY PLEASE BRING IT BACK OR FURTHER STEPS WILL BE TAKEN

- HORSE MANURE PER PRE-PACKED BAG DO-IT-YOURSELF

- AFTER TEA BREAK STAFF SHOULD EMPTY THE TEAPOT AND STAND UPSIDE DOWN ON THE DRAINING BOARD

- THIS IS THE GATE OF HEAVEN. ENTER YE ALL BY THIS DOOR. (THIS DOOR IS KEPT LOCKED BECAUSE OF THE DRAFT. PLEASE USE SIDE DOOR.)

- WE EXCHANGE ANYTHING - BICYCLES, WASHING MACHINES, ETC. WHY NOT BRING YOUR WIFE ALONG AND GET A WONDERFUL BARGAIN?

- THE TOWN HALL IS CLOSED UNTIL OPENING. IT WILL REMAIN CLOSED AFTER BEING OPENED. OPEN TOMORROW.

- OUT TO LUNCH: IF NOT BACK BY FIVE, OUT FOR DINNER ALSO.

- SLOW CATTLE CROSSING. NO OVERTAKING FOR THE NEXT 100 YRS.

- SMARTS IS THE MOST EXCLUSIVE DISCO IN TOWN. EVERYONE WELCOME.

- DUE TO INCREASING PROBLEMS WITH LETTERLOUTS AND VANDALS WE MUST ASK ANYONE WITH RELATIVES BURIED IN THE GRAVEYARD TO DO THEIR BEST TO KEEP THEM IN ORDER.

- ANYONE LEAVING THEIR GARMENTS HERE FOR MORE THAN 30 DAYS WILL BE DISPOSED OF.

- PLEASE DO NOT SMOKE NEAR OUR PETROL PUMPS. YOUR LIFE MAY NOT BE WORTH MUCH BUT OUR PETROL IS.

- ELEPHANTS PLEASE STAY IN YOUR CAR.

- FOR ANYONE WHO HAS CHILDREN AND DOESN'T KNOW IT, THERE IS A DAY CARE ON THE FIRST FLOOR.

- THE FARMER ALLOWS WALKERS TO CROSS THE FIELD FOR FREE, BUT THE BULL CHARGES.

- IF YOU CANNOT READ, THIS LEAFLET WILL TELL YOU HOW TO GET LESSONS.

- WE CAN REPAIR ANYTHING. (PLEASE KNOCK HARD ON THE DOOR - THE BELL DOESN'T WORK).

- BEWARE! I SHOOT EVERY TENTH TRESPASSER AND THE NINTH ONE HAS JUST LEFT.

Missing the Obvious

One day a diver was enjoying the aquatic world 20 ft below sea level. He noticed a guy at the same depth he was, but he had on no scuba gear whatsoever.

The diver went below another 20 ft, but the guy joined him a few moments later. The diver went below still another 25 ft, but soon the same guy joined him. This confused the diver, so he took out a waterproof chalk-and-board set, and wrote,

"How on earth are you able to stay under this deep without equipment?"

The guy took the board and chalk, erased what the diver had written, and wrote,

"I'M DROWNING, YOU GOOBER!!!"

Tips from Cowboys

- Never squat with your spurs on!

- Never kick a fresh cow chip on a hot day.

- There's two theories to arguin' with a woman. Neither one works.

- Don't worry about bitin' off more than you can chew. Your mouth is probably a whole lot bigger than you think.

- If you get to thinkin' you're a person of some influence, try orderin' somebody else's dog around.

- After eating an entire bull, a mountain lion felt so good he started roaring. He kept it up until a hunter came along and shot him. The moral: When you're full of bull, keep your mouth shut.

- If you find yourself in a hole, the first thing to do is stop diggin'.

- Never smack a man who's chewin' tobacco.

- It don't take a genius to spot a goat in a flock of sheep.

- Never ask a barber if he thinks you need a haircut.

- Good judgment comes from experience, and a lot of that comes from bad judgment.

- Always drink upstream from the herd.

- Never drop your gun to hug a grizzly.

- If you're ridin' ahead of the herd, take a look back every now and then to make sure it's still there.

- When you give a lesson in meanness to a critter or a person, don't be surprised if they learn their lesson.

- When you're throwin' your weight around, be ready to have it thrown around by somebody else.

- Lettin' the cat outta the bag is a whole lot easier than puttin' it back.

- Always take a good look at what you're about to eat. It's not so important to know what it is, but it's critical to know what it was.

- The quickest way to double your money is to fold it over and put it back in your pocket.

- Never miss a good chance to shut up.

Seeing Eye Dogs

Two men are walking their dogs. The first guy has a Doberman, and the second guy has a Chihuahua. They walk down the street and stop at a restaurant.

"Man, I could really go for a pop," says the first guy.

"So could I, but the sign says No Dogs Allowed," says the second guy.

So the first guy says, "Wait here, I have an idea!"

The first guy with the Doberman puts on his sunglasses and walks into the restaurant and asks for a drink, and the waiter says, "Hey, no dogs allowed. Didn't you read the sign?"

The guy replies, "No, I didn't. I'm blind and this is my Seeing Eye dog." The waiter apologizes and serves him his drink.

The second guy watches all this, puts on his sunglasses and goes in. The waiter again says, "Hey, no dogs allowed. Didn't you read the sign?"

The guy with the Chihuahua replies, "No, I didn't. I'm blind, and this is my Seeing Eye dog."

The bartender exclaims, "What! That little Chihuahua?"

The second guy replies, "WHAT! They gave me a Chihuahua?!"

Actual Headings

Actual Newspaper Headlines (collected by journalists)

Police Begin Campaign To Run Down Jaywalkers

Safety Experts Say School Bus Passengers Should Be Belted

Drunk Gets Nine Months In Violin Case

Survivor Of Siamese Twins Joins Parents

Farmer Bill Dies In House

Iraqi Head Seeks Arms

Soviet Virgin Lands Short Of Goal Again

British Left Waffles On Falkland Islands

Lung Cancer In Women Mushrooms

Eye Drops Off Shelf

Teacher Strikes Idle Kids

Reagan Wins On Budget, But More Lies Ahead

Squad Helps Dog Bite Victim

Shot Off Woman's Leg Helps Nicklaus To 66

Enraged Cow Injures Farmer with Ax

Plane Too Close To Ground, Crash Probe Told

Miners Refuse to Work After Death

Juvenile Court To Try Shooting Defendant

Stolen Painting Found By Tree

Two Soviet Ships Collide, One Dies

Two Sisters Reunited After 18 Years In Checkout Counter

Killer Sentenced To Die For Second Time In 10 Years

Drunken Drivers Paid $1000 in '84

War Dims Hope For Peace

If Strike Isn't Settled Quickly, It May Last a While

Cold Wave Linked To Temperatures

Enfields Couple Slain; Police Suspect Homicide

RED TAPE HOLDS UP NEW BRIDGE

DEER KILL 17,000

TYPHOON RIPS THROUGH CEMETERY; HUNDREDS DEAD

MAN STRUCK BY LIGHTNING FACES BATTERY CHARGE

NEW STUDY OF OBESITY LOOKS FOR LARGER TEST GROUP

ASTRONAUT TAKES BLAME FOR GAS IN SPACECRAFT

KIDS MAKE NUTRITIOUS SNACKS

CHEF THROWS HIS HEART INTO HELPING NEEDY

ARSON SUSPECT IS HELD IN MASSACHUSETTS FIRE

BRITISH UNION FINDS DWARVES IN SHORT SUPPLY

BAN ON SOLICITING DEAD IN TROTWOOD

LANSING RESIDENTS CAN DROP OFF TREES

LOCAL HIGH SCHOOL DROPOUTS CUT IN HALF

NEW VACCINE MAY CONTAIN RABIES

MAN MINUS EAR WAIVES HEARING

DEAF COLLEGE OPENS DOORS TO HEARING

AIR HEAD FIRED

STEALS CLOCK, FACES TIME

OLD SCHOOL PILLARS ARE REPLACED BY ALUMNI

BANK DRIVE-IN WINDOW BLOCKED BY BOARD

HOSPITALS ARE SUED BY 7 FOOT DOCTORS

SEX EDUCATION DELAYED, TEACHERS REQUEST TRAINING

INCLUDE YOUR CHILDREN WHEN BAKING COOKIES

POLICE DISCOVERED POT PLANTS WERE REALLY CANNABIS

Photo Radar – A Picture Is Not Worth Much In The Eyes Of The Law

A motorist was unknowingly caught in an automated speed trap that measured his speed using radar and photographed his car.

He later received in the mail, a ticket for $40.00, and a photo of his car. Instead of the payment, he sent the police department a photograph of two $20.00 bills.

Several days later, he received a letter from the police department that contained another picture, of a pair of handcuffs.

McDonald's Job Application

This is an actual job application someone submitted at a McDonald's fast-food establishment........ and they hired him! As what?

1. NAME: Greg Bulmash

2. DESIRED POSITION: Reclining. Ha ha. But seriously, whatever's available. If I was in a position to be picky, I wouldn't be applying here in the first place.

3. DESIRED SALARY: $185,000 a year plus stock options and a Michael Ovitz style severance package. If that's not possible, make an offer and we can haggle.

4. EDUCATION: Yes.

5. LAST POSITION HELD: Target for middle management hostility.

6. SALARY: Less than I'm worth.

7. MOST NOTABLE ACHIEVEMENT: My collection of stolen pens.

8. REASON FOR LEAVING: It sucked.

9. HOURS AVAILABLE TO WORK: Any.

10. PREFERRED HOURS: 1:30-3:30 p.m., Monday, Tuesday, and Thursday.

11. MAY WE CONTACT YOUR CURRENT EMPLOYER?: If I had one, would I be here?

12. DO YOU HAVE ANY PHYSICAL CONDITIONS THAT WOULD PROHIBIT YOU FROM LIFTING (UP TO 50 LBS)?: Of what?

13. DO YOU HAVE A CAR?: I think the more appropriate question here would be, "Do you have a car that runs?"

14. HAVE YOU RECEIVED ANY SPECIAL AWARDS OR RECOGNITION?: I may already be a winner of the Publishers Clearinghouse Sweepstakes.

15. DO YOU SMOKE?: Only when set on fire.

16. WHAT WOULD YOU LIKE TO BE DOING IN FIVE YEARS?: Living in the Bahamas with a fabulously

wealthy super model who thinks I'm the greatest thing since sliced bread. Actually, I'd like to be doing that now.

17.   DO YOU CERTIFY THAT THE ABOVE IS TRUE AND COMPLETE TO THE BEST OF YOUR KNOWLEDGE?: No, but I dare you to prove otherwise.

Goober Ice Fishing

A goober wanted to go ice fishing. She'd seen many books on the subject, and finally, after getting all the necessary "tools" together, she made for the nearest frozen lake.

After positioning her comfy footstool, she started to make a circular cut in the ice. Suddenly, from the sky, a voice boomed, "THERE ARE NO FISH UNDER THE ICE!"

Startled, the goober moved further down the ice, poured a thermos of cappuccino, and began to cut yet another hole. Again, from the heavens, the voice bellowed, "THERE ARE NO FISH UNDER THE ICE!"

The goober, now quite worried, moved way down to the opposite end of the ice, set up her stool, and tried again to cut her hole. The voice came once more. "THERE ARE NO FISH UNDER THE ICE!"

She stopped, looked skyward, and said, "Is that you, Lord?"

The voice replied, "NO, THIS IS THE MANAGER OF THE ICE RINK!"

Banff Park Tourist Questions

Here are some of the "All Time Dumbest Questions Asked by Banff Park Tourists"

ON NATURE...

How do the elk know they're supposed to cross at the "Elk Crossing" signs?

At what elevation does an elk become a moose?

Tourist: "How do you pronounce 'Elk'?" Park Information Staff: "'Elk.'" Tourist: "Oh."

Are the bears with collars tame?

Is there anywhere I can see the bears pose?

Is it okay to keep an open bag of bacon on the picnic table, or should I store it in my tent?

Where can I find Alpine Flamingos?

I saw an animal on the way to Banff today - could you tell me what it was?

Are there birds in Canada?

ON GEOGRAPHY...

Did I miss the turnoff for Canada? (while standing in the middle of Banff!)

Where does Alberta end and Canada begin?

Do you have a map of the State of Jasper?

Is this the part of Canada that speaks French, or is that Saskatchewan?

If I go to B.C., do I have to go through Ontario?

Which is the way to the Columbia Rice fields?

How far is Banff from Canada?

What's the best way to see Canada in a day?

ON TOURIST FACILITIES...

Do they search you at the B.C. border?

When we enter B.C. do we have to convert our money to British pounds?

Where can I buy a raccoon hat? ALL Canadians own one don't they?

Are there phones in Banff?

So it's eight kilometers away... is that in miles? We're on the decibel system you know.

Where can I get my husband really, REALLY, lost??

Is that 2 kilometers by foot or by car?

Don't you Canadians know anything?

Temperance River

A preacher was completing a temperance sermon. With great expression he said, "If I had all the beer in the world, I'd take it and throw it into the river."

With even greater emphasis he said, "And if I had all the wine in the world, I'd take it and throw it into the river."

And then finally, he said, "And if I had all the whisky in the world, I'd take it and throw it into the river." He sat down.

The song leader then stood very cautiously and announced with a smile, "For our closing song, let us sing Hymn #365: 'Shall We Gather at the River.'"

Quotable Quotes

I stopped believing in Santa Claus when my mother took me to see him in a department store, and he asked for my autograph. --*Shirley Temple*

If all the cars in the United States were placed end to end, it would probably be Labor Day Weekend. --*Doug Lars*

A bank is a place that will lend you money if you can prove that you don't need it. --*Bob Hope*

I know that there are people in this world who do not love their fellow man, and I hate people like that! --*Tom Lehrer*

I was going to buy a copy of The Power of Positive Thinking, and then I thought: What good would that do? --*Ronnie Shakes*

It is difficult to produce a television documentary that is both incisive and probing when every twelve minutes one is interrupted by dancing rabbits singing about toilet paper. --*Rod Serling*

Somewhere on this globe, every ten seconds, there is a woman giving birth to a child. She must be found and stopped. --*Sam Levenson (1911-1980)*

Television - a medium. So called because it is neither rare nor well-done. --*Ernie Kovacs*

Always remember this: If you don't attend the funerals of your friends, they will certainly not attend yours. --*H.L. Mencken*

A good novel tells us the truth about its hero; but a bad novel tells us the truth about its author. --*G. K. Chesterton (1874-1936)*

Thus the metric system did not really catch on in the United States, unless you count the increasing popularity of the nine-milimeter bullet. --*Dave Barry*

This isn't right. It isn't even wrong. --*Wolfgang Pauli, on a paper submitted by a physicist colleague*

Today you can go to a gas station and find the cash register open and the toilets locked. They must think toilet paper is worth more than money. --*Joey Bishop*

The trouble with being punctual is that nobody's there to appreciate it. -- *Franklin P. Jones*

Red meat is NOT bad for you. Now, blue-green meat, that's REALLY BAD for you. --*Tommy Smothers*

When you go into court you are putting your fate into the hands of twelve people who weren't smart enough to get out of jury duty. --*Norm Crosby*

The imaginary friends I had as a kid dropped me because their friends thought I didn't exist. --*Aaron Machado*

I told the doctor I broke my leg in two places. He told me to quit going to those places. --*Henny Youngman*

The reason there are two senators for each state is so that one can be the designated driver. --*Jay Leno*

It matters not whether you win or lose; what matters is whether I win or lose. --*Darrin Weinberg*

Remember that as a teenager you are in the last stage of your life in which you will be happy to hear that the phone is for you. --*Fran Lebowitz*

A cynic is a man who, when he smells flowers, looks around for a coffin. --*H.L. Mencken*

It ain't so much the things you don't know that get you in trouble. It's the things you know that just ain't so. --*Artimus Ward, 1834-1867*

Goober Horseback Riding

A goober decides to try horseback riding, even though he has had no lessons or prior experience. He mounts the horse unassisted and the horse immediately springs into motion.

It gallops along at a steady and rhythmic pace, but the goober begins to slip from the saddle. In terror, he grabs for the horse's mane, but cannot seem to get a firm grip. He tries to throw his arms around the horse's neck, but he slides down the side of the horse anyway.

The horse gallops along, seemingly impervious to its slipping rider. Finally, giving up his frail grip, he leaps away from the horse to try and throw himself to safety.

Unfortunately, his foot has become entangled in the stirrup and he is now at the mercy of the horse's pounding hooves as his head is struck against the ground again and again. As his head is battered against the ground, he is mere moments away from unconsciousness when...

the Wal-Mart manager runs out to shut the horse off.

Steeple Paint

The church steeple in Port Gibson is very high, and was being painted on a rather hot day. The painter was about halfway down and, as the steeple was widening out, was taking more and more paint. The painter felt that he might not have enough paint to finish. Since he was hot and tired, and did not care to make another trip to the ground, he decided to stretch the amount of paint by adding some paint thinner to it.

When finished, he lowered himself to the ground and went about cleaning up. Then he looked up to see the results of his work and noted that the area with the thinned paint looked decidedly different. He was pondering about what to do about it when the sky turned dark and there was a lightning flash and loud thunderclap. Then in a loud, booming voice from the sky came the words,

"REPAINT AND THIN NO MORE!"

Isn't Aging Fun!

Do you realize that the only time in our lives when we like to get old is when we're kids?

If you're less than 10 years old, you're so excited about aging that you think in fractions. How old are you? "I'm four and a half." You're never 36 and a half.... you're four and a half going on five!

That's the key. You get into your teens, and now they can't hold you back. You jump to the next number. How old are you? "I'm gonna be 16." You could be 12, but you're gonna be 16.

And then the greatest day of your life happens - you become 21. Even the words sound like a ceremony. You BECOME 21...YES!!!

But then you turn 30.... ooohhh what happened there? Makes you sound like bad milk. He TURNED; we had to throw him out. There's no fun now.

What's wrong?? What changed?? You BECOME 21, you TURN 30, then you're PUSHING 40... stay over there, it's all slipping away...

You BECOME 21, you TURN 30, you're PUSHING 40, you REACH 50...and your dreams are gone.

Then you MAKE IT to 60...you didn't think you'd make it!!!!

So you BECOME 21, you TURN 30, you're PUSHING 40, you REACH 50, you MAKE IT to 60... then you build up so much speed you HIT 70!

After that, it's a day-by-day thing. After that, you HIT Wednesday....

You get into your 80's, you HIT lunch. My grandmother won't even buy green bananas... it's an investment you know, and maybe a bad one.

And it doesn't end there.... into the 90's you start going backwards.... I was JUST 92...

Then a strange thing happens. If you make it over 100, you become a little kid again...."I'm 100 and a half!!!!"

Who Said That?

If quitters never win, and winners never quit, what fool came up with "Quit while you're ahead"?

What hair color do they put on the driver's licenses of bald men?

I thought about how mothers feed their babies with little tiny spoons and forks, so I wonder what Chinese mothers use. Perhaps toothpicks?

Why do they put pictures of criminals up in the Post Office? What are we supposed to do...write to them? Why don't they just put their pictures on the postage stamps so mailmen can look for them while they deliver the mail?

If it's true that we are here to help others, then what exactly are the OTHERS here for?

STRESSED spelled backwards is DESSERTS.

Clones are people two.

No one ever says "It's only a game" when their team is winning.

As I said before, I never repeat myself!

If you can't be kind, at least have the decency to be vague.

Ever wonder what the speed of lightning would be if it didn't zigzag?

Nostalgia isn't what it used to be.

It's hard to make a comeback when you haven't been anywhere.

Truth About Children

A baby usually wakes up in the wee-wee hours of the morning.

A child will not spill on a dirty floor.

A young child is a noise with dirt on it.

86

A youth becomes a man when the marks he wants to leave on the world have nothing to do with tires.

An unbreakable toy is useful for breaking other toys.

Be nice to your kids, for it is they who will choose your nursing home.

Celibacy is not hereditary.

Familiarity breeds children.

For adult education, nothing beats children.

Having children is like having a bowling alley installed in your brain.

Having children will turn you into your parents.

If you have trouble getting your children's attention, just sit down and look comfortable.

Ill-bred children always display their pest manners.

It now costs more to amuse a child than it did to educate his father.

It rarely occurs to teenagers that the day will come when they'll know as little as their parents.

Money isn't everything, but it sure keeps the kids in touch.

Never lend your car to anyone to whom you have given birth.

You can learn many things from children... like how much patience you have.

Summer vacation is a time when parents realize that teachers are grossly underpaid.

The first sign of maturity is the discovery that the volume knob also turns to the left.

There are three ways to get things done: 1) do it yourself 2) hire someone to do it 3) forbid your kids to do it.

Those who say they "sleep like a baby" haven't got one.

There would be fewer problems with children if they had to chop wood to keep the television set going.

The best thing to spend on your children is time.

I Just Can't Drive Today

For the second time in a row, I was forced to impose on the woman with whom I carpooled to our children's soccer practice.

I phoned and explained that my husband had the car again, so I wouldn't be able to take my turn. A few minutes before she was due to pick up my son, my husband showed up. Since it was too late for me to call and say I could drive after all, I asked my husband to hide the car in the garage and to stay inside. I also explained to my son that he shouldn't mention anything about his father's whereabouts.

Unfortunately, my husband forgot and was in front of our house chatting with a friend when my carpool partner arrived. When my son returned from practice, I asked him if she had noticed.

"Yes," he replied, "she asked me which of the two men in front of the house was my father. But don't worry. I told her I didn't know."

Stupid Inventions

Black Highlighter

Braille Driver's Manual

Clear Correction Fluid

Fake Rhinestones

Inflatable Dart Board

Mesh Umbrella

Motorcycle Air Conditioner

Sugar Coated Toothpaste

Super-glue Post-it Notes

First Time Sky Diver

A man goes skydiving for the first time.

After listening to the instructor for what seems like days, he is ready to go. Excited, he jumps out of the plane. After a bit, he pulls the ripcord. Nothing happens. He tries again. Still nothing. He starts to panic, but remembers his back-up chute. He pulls that cord. Nothing happens. He frantically begins pulling both cords, but to no avail.

Suddenly, he looks down and he can't believe his eyes. Another man is in the air with him, but this guy is going up! Just as the other guy passes by, the skydiver, by this time scared out of his wits, yells, "Hey, do you know anything about skydiving?"

The other guy yells back, "No! Do you know anything about gas stoves?"

I'm Not Old...Just Mature

Today at the drugstore, the clerk was a gent.

From my purchase this chap took off ten percent.

I asked for the cause of a lesser amount;

And he answered, "Because of the Seniors Discount."

I went to McDonald's for a burger and fries;

And there, once again, got quite a surprise.

The clerk poured some coffee, which he handed to me.

He said, "For you, Seniors, the coffee is free."

Understand---I'm not old---I'm merely mature;

But some things are changing, temporarily, I'm sure.

The newspaper print gets smaller each day,

And people speak softer---can't hear what they say.

My teeth are my own (I have the receipt),

and my glasses identify people I meet.

Oh, I've slowed down a bit...not a lot, I am sure.

You see, I'm not old...I'm only mature.

The gold in my hair has been bleached by the sun.

You should see all the damage that chlorine has done.

Washing my hair has turned it all white,

But don't call it gray...saying "blond" is just right.

My car is all paid for...not a nickel is owed.

Yet a kid yells, "Old duffer...get off of the road!"

My car has no scratches...not even a dent.

Still I get all that guff from a punk who's "Hell bent."

My friends all get older...much faster than me.

They seem much more wrinkled, from what I can see.

I've got "character lines," not wrinkles...for sure,

But don't call me old...just call me mature.

The steps in the houses they're building today

Are so high that they take...your breath all away;

And the streets are much steeper than ten years ago.

That should explain why my walking is slow.

But I'm keeping up on what's hip and what's new,

And I think I can still dance a mean boogaloo.

I'm still in the running...in this I'm secure,

I'm not really old...I'm only mature.

Author Unknown

The Truth About The Home Handyman's Tools

HAMMER:

Originally employed as a weapon of war, the hammer nowadays is used as a kind of divining rod to locate expensive parts not far from the object we are trying to hit.

MECHANIC'S KNIFE:

Used to open and slice through the contents of cardboard cartons delivered to your front door; works particularly well on boxes containing seats and motorcycle jackets.

ELECTRIC HAND DRILL:

Normally used for spinning steel Pop rivets in their holes until you die of old age, but it also works great for drilling mounting holes in fenders just above the brake line that goes to the rear wheel.

PLIERS:

Used to round off bolt heads.

HACKSAW:

One of a family of cutting tools built on the original sin principle. It transforms human energy into a crooked, unpredictable motion, and the more you attempt to influence its course, the more dismal your future becomes.

VISE-GRIPS:

Used to round off bolt heads. If nothing else is available, they can also be used to transfer intense welding heat to the palm of your hand.

OXYACETYLENE TORCH:

Used almost entirely for lighting various flammable objects in your garage on fire. Also handy for igniting the grease inside a brake drum you're trying to get the bearing race out of.

WHITWORTH SOCKETS:

Once used for working on older British cars and motorcycles, they are now used mainly for impersonating that 9/16 or 1/2 socket you've been searching for the last 15 minutes.

DRILL PRESS:

A tall upright machine useful for suddenly snatching flat metal bar stock out of your hands so that it smacks you in the chest and flings your coffee across the room, splattering it against that freshly painted part you were drying.

WIRE WHEEL:

Cleans rust off old bolts and then throws them somewhere under the workbench with the speed of light. Also removes fingerprint whorls and hard-earned guitar calluses in about the time it takes you to say, "Ouc...."

HYDRAULIC FLOOR JACK:

Used for lowering a motorcycle to the ground after you have installed your new front disk brake setup, trapping the jack handle firmly under the front fender.

EIGHT-FOOT LONG DOUGLAS FIR 2X4:

Used for levering a motorcycle upward off a hydraulic jack.

TWEEZERS:

A tool for removing wood splinters.

PHONE:

Tool for calling your neighbor to see if he has another hydraulic floor jack.

SNAP-ON GASKET SCRAPER:

Theoretically useful as a sandwich tool for spreading mayonnaise; used mainly for getting dog-doo off your boot.

E-Z OUT BOLT AND STUD EXTRACTOR:

A tool that snaps off in bolt holes and is ten times harder than any known drill bit.

TIMING LIGHT:

A stroboscopic instrument for illuminating grease buildup.

TWO-TON HYDRAULIC ENGINE HOIST:

A handy tool for testing the tensile strength of ground straps and brake lines you may have forgotten to disconnect.

CRAFTSMAN 1/2 x 16-INCH SCREWDRIVER:

A large motor mount prying tool that inexplicably has an accurately machined screwdriver tip on the end without the handle.

BATTERY ELECTROLYTE TESTER:

A handy tool for transferring sulfuric acid from a car battery to the inside of your toolbox after determining that your battery is dead as a doornail, just as you thought.

TROUBLE LIGHT:

The mechanic's own tanning booth. Sometimes called a drop light, it is a good source of vitamin D, "the sunshine vitamin," which is not otherwise found under motorcycles at night. Health benefits aside, its main purpose is to consume 40-watt light bulbs at about the same rate that 105-mm howitzer shells might be used during, say, the first few hours of the Battle of the Bulge. More often dark than light, its name is somewhat misleading.

PHILLIPS SCREWDRIVER:

Normally used to stab the lids of old-style paper-and-tin oil cans and splash oil on your shirt; can also be used, as the name implies, to round off Phillips screw heads.

AIR COMPRESSOR:

A machine that takes energy produced in a coal-burning power plant 200 miles away and transforms it into compressed air that travels by hose to a Chicago Pneumatic impact wrench that grips rusty bolts last tightened 40 years ago by someone in Sindelfingen, and rounds them off.

PRY BAR:

A tool used to crumple the metal surrounding that clip or bracket you needed to remove in order to replace a 50-cent part.

One Little Square

A little boy returning home from his first day at school said to his mother, "Mum, what's sex?"

His mother, who believed in all the most modern educational theories, gave him a detailed explanation, covering all aspects of the tricky subject.

When she had finished, the little lad produced an enrolment form, which he had brought home from school and said,

"Yes, but how am I going to get all that into this one little square?"

Elderly Couple Sharing

A young man saw an elderly couple sitting down to lunch at McDonald's. He noticed that they had ordered one meal, and an extra drink cup.

As he watched, the gentleman carefully divided the hamburger in half, then counted out the fries, one for him, one for her, until each had half of them.

Then he poured half of the soft drink into the extra cup and set that in front of his wife.

The old man then began to eat, and his wife sat watching, with her hands folded in her lap. The young man decided to ask if they would allow him to purchase another meal for them so that they didn't have to split theirs.

The old gentleman said, "Oh, no. We've been married 50 years, and everything has always been and will always be shared, 50-50."

The young man then asked the wife if she was going to eat, and she replied, "Not yet. It's his turn with the teeth."

The Friars of Flowers

Some friars were behind in their belfry payments, so they opened a small florist shop to raise funds. Since everyone liked to buy flowers from the men of God, a rival florist across town thought the competition was unfair.

He asked the good fathers to close down, but they would not. He went back and begged the friars to close. They ignored him. He asked his mother to go ask the friars to get out of business. They ignored her. So, the rival florist hired Hugh MacTaggart, the roughest and most vicious thug in town to "persuade" them to close. Hugh beat up the friars and trashed their store, saying he'd be back if they didn't close shop. Terrified, the friars did so. The moral of the story: Wait for it....

Hugh, and only Hugh, can prevent florist friars!!

Navajo Wisdom

About 1969 or so, a NASA team doing work for the Apollo moon mission took the astronauts near Tuba City where the terrain of the Navajo Reservation looks very much like the Lunar surface. Along with all the trucks and large vehicles, there were two large figures dressed in full Lunar spacesuits.

Nearby a Navajo sheep herder and his son were watching the strange creatures walk about, occasionally being tended by personnel. The two Navajo people were noticed and approached by the NASA personnel. Since the man did not know English, his son asked for him what the strange creatures were and the NASA people told them that they are just men that are getting ready to go to the moon. The man became very excited and asked if he could send a message to the moon with the astronauts. The NASA personnel thought this was a great idea so they rustled up a tape recorder. After the man gave them his message, they asked his son to translate. His son would not.

Later, they tried a few more people on the reservation to translate and every person they asked would chuckle and then refuse to translate. Finally, with cash in hand, someone translated the message, "Watch out for these guys, they come to take your land."

Information Assistance?

"Information. Can I help you?"

"I'd like the number of the Theater Guild, please."

"One moment, please." Pause. "I'm sorry sir, I have no listing for a Theodore Guild."

"No, no. It isn't a person. It's an organization. It's Theater Guild."

"I told you, sir. I have no listing for a Theodore Guild."

"Not *Theodore*! *Theater*! The word is *theater*. T-H-E-A-T-E-R!"

"That, *sir*, is NOT the way you spell Theodore."

Because I'm a Guy

I must hold the television remote control in my hand while I watch TV. If the thing has been misplaced, I'll miss a whole show looking for it, though one time I was able to survive by holding a calculator.

When I lock my keys in the car, I will fiddle with a wire clothes hanger and ignore your suggestions that we call road service until long after hypothermia has set in. Oh, and when the car isn't running very well, I will pop the hood and stare at the engine as if I know what I'm looking at. If another guy shows up, one of us will say to the other, "I used to be able to fix these things, but now with all these computers and everything, I wouldn't know where to start."

94

When I catch a cold I need someone to bring me soup and take care of me while I lie in bed and moan. You never get as sick as I do, so for you this isn't an issue.

I can be relied upon to purchase basic groceries at the store, like milk, or bread. I cannot be expected to find exotic items like "Cumin" or "Tofu." For all I know these are the same thing. And never, under any circumstances, expect me to pick up a copy of "Cosmo" or "Better Homes & Gardens."

When one of our appliances stops working, I will insist on taking it apart, despite evidence that this will just cost me twice as much once the repair person gets here and has to put it back together.

I don't think we're all that lost, and no, I don't think we should stop and ask someone. Why would you listen to a complete stranger--how could HE know where we're going?

You don't have to ask me if I liked the movie. Chances are, if you're crying at the end of it, I didn't.

I think what you're wearing is fine. I thought what you were wearing five minutes ago was fine, too. Either pair of shoes is fine. With the belt or without it looks fine. Your hair is fine. You look fine. Can we just go now?

Diary of A House Husband

This week I am at home and playing house husband. My wife left a list of things I need to do. This is soooooo easy I thought I would share it with you.

1. Make the beds.
    What a waste of effort, we're only going to sleep in them again tonight. Forget that. Scratch one.

2. Pick up dog poop in yard.
    It snowed last night, I don't see any dog poop. Kids do you see any dog poop? Scratch two.

3. Drop your shirts off at the cleaners.
    Duhh. I'm on vacation I don't need them. Scratch three. This is easy, what's the fuss. Think I'll go on the computer for a while.

4. Clean out Tupperware cabinet.
    Uhhhh that's a hard one. GOT IT! Velcro on the doors will keep them closed. Scratch four.

5. Mop kitchen floor.
    The dog licked up that sugar spill from breakfast, floor

looks clean to me. Scratch five. Good doggie, go play in the yard.
She just loves rolling in the snow.

6. Find something fun for the kids to do.
    That tinfoil in the microwave thing was kinda fun. Scratch six. This
    is way too easy. I'll have lots of time for the computer.

7. Vacuum the carpets.
    That's a hard one. Hey kids wanna have some more FUN? Scratch
    seven.

8. Feed kids lunch.
    Hey kids, don't you have a friend's house to go to? YESSSS.
    Scratch eight!!

9. Clean out hallway closet.
    Hmmmm, another hard one. That's it, take enough out of the closet
    to close the door. Outta sight, outta mind. Hmmmm this other stuff
    can go under a bed. Scratch nine. Boy o boy am I good.
    Lunchtime. Pour some chili into the cracker bag and eat. Taaa daaa.
    No lunch dishes.

10. Do laundry.
    No problem I can do that while I'm on the computer. Scratch ten.

11. Fold laundry.
    Wow! Ya know I never noticed how many pink things this family
    actually wears. Gonna have to ask the little lady why she buys me
    pale pink underwear!? Check this out! A cashmere Barbie sweater,
    cool.   Scratch eleven.

12. Put the laundry away.
    Baskets in bedrooms work for me. Scratch twelve. This is way too
    easy. Wonder why women always complain about housework???

13. Water the Christmas tree.
    Ooop's good thing the carpet is absorbent. Scratch thirteen.

14. Grocery shopping, buy toilet paper.
    These old newspapers will do, besides, that's recycling and that's
    good for the earth.... Scratch fourteen.

15. Pick up the kids.
    Yeah right, we're talking about my kids here. Parents will normally
    pay to drop them back off. They'll be back. Scratch fifteen. Wonder
    who's on the computer? I have plenty of time.

16. Make dinner.
    Easy, "Hello do you deliver? Uhhh double that, ya know we will need
    more dinner tomorrow". Scratch sixteen.

17. Clean out the dog's house.
    Duhh. The dog sleeps in our bed, like that needs to be done.
    Scratch seventeen.

WOW all done. Still time for some more computer and a nap.......Man
this is sooooo easy.

Cake Baking for Mom's of Small Children

Preheat oven, get out utensils and ingredients.

Remove blocks and toy cars from table.

Grease pan, crack nuts.

Measure two cups flour.

Remove baby's hands from flour, wash flour off baby.

Remeasure flour.

Put flour, baking powder, and salt in sifter.

Get dustpan and brush up pieces of bowl baby knocked on floor.

Get another bowl.

Answer doorbell.

Return to kitchen.

Remove baby's hands from bowl.

Wash baby.

Answer phone.

Return.

Remove 1/4-inch salt from greased pan.

Look for baby.

Grease another pan.

Answer telephone.

Return to kitchen and find baby.

Remove baby's hands from bowl.

Take up greased pan, find layer of nutshells in it.

Head for baby, who flees, knocking bowl off table.

Wash kitchen floor, table, wall, and dishes.

97

Call baker.

Lie down.

Waking Up Mad

One day a man took the train from Paris to Frankfurt. When he got on he said to the ticket man, "Sir, I really need you to do me a favor. I have to get off this train in Mannheim, but I'm very tired and it is certain that I will fall asleep. So I want you to wake me up in Mannheim because I have to close a business deal there and it is very important. Here, you have 100 francs for the favor. But I warn you, sometimes when people wake me up I get really violent, but no matter what I do or say you have to get me off this train in Mannheim. Is that clear?" So the ticket man agreed and took the 100 francs.

Later, as the man had said, he fell asleep. When he woke up he realized that he was in Frankfurt. He was so mad that he ran over and started yelling at the ticket man. "Are you STUPID or something??? I paid you 100 francs so that you would wake me up in Mannheim and you didn't! I want my money back." While he was yelling at the ticket man, two other guys on the train were looking at them. One turned to the other and said to him:

Guy1: "Look at this guy. He is mad!"

Guy2: "Yeah, almost as mad as the guy they made get off the train in Mannheim."

Keeping Warm

Chevy has added wires to the rear window to clear fog and frost.

Dodge is adding wires under the wipers so they can be freed when frozen and not burn up the motor.

But Ford is adding the wire elements to the tailgates on all of their trucks to keeps your hands warm while you're pushing!

You Know You're Really a Mom When...

- You count the sprinkles on each kid's cupcake to make sure they're equal.

- You want to take out a contract on the kid who broke your child's favorite toy and made him/her cry.

- You have time to shave only one leg at a time.

- You hide in the bathroom to be alone.

- Your child throws up and you catch it.

- Someone else's kid throws up at a party and you keep eating.

- You consider finger paint to be a controlled substance.

- You mastered the art of placing food on a plate without anything touching.

- Your child insists that you read "Once Upon a Potty" out loud in the lobby of the doctor's office, and you do it.

- You hire a sitter because you haven't been out with your husband in ages, and then spend half the night talking about and checking on the kids.

- You hope ketchup is a vegetable because it's the only one your child eats.

- You can't bear the thought of your son's first girlfriend.

- You hate the thought of his wife even more.

- You find yourself cutting your husband's sandwiches into unusual shapes.

- You fast-forward through the scene when the hunter shoots Bambi's mother.

- You obsess when your child clings to you upon parting during his first month at school, then obsess when he finally skips in without looking back.

- You can't bear to give away baby clothes--it's so final.

- You hear your mother's voice coming out of your mouth when you say, "Not in your good clothes."

- You stop criticizing the way your mother raised you.

- You read that the average five-year-old asks 437 questions a day and feel proud that your kid is "above average."

- You say at least once a day, "I'm not cut out for this job," but you know you wouldn't trade it for anything.

Lemon Aid

A local bar was so sure its bartender was the strongest man around that they offered a $1000 bet that the bartender could squeeze a lemon so dry no one could get another drop out. Many people tried but no one was ever able to succeed.

One day a puny little man wearing a polyester suit and glasses came in and said, "I'd like to try the bet". After the laughter died down, the bartender grabbed the lemon and squeezed it until it was as dry as the desert.

The little man took the wrinkled remains and clenched it in his small fist, the crowd's laughter turned to silence as six drops of juice fell.

"What do you do for a living?" the crowd asked. "I work for Revenue Canada" the little man replied!

Today I Didn't Do It

One afternoon a man came home from work to find total mayhem in his house. His three children were outside, still in their pajamas, playing in the mud, with empty food boxes and wrappers strewn all around the front yard. The door of his wife's car was open, as was the front door to the house.

Proceeding into the entry, he found an even bigger mess. A lamp had been knocked over, and the throw rug was wadded against one wall. In the front room the TV was loudly blaring a cartoon channel, and the family room was strewn with toys and various items of clothing. In the kitchen, dishes filled the sink, breakfast food was spilled on the counter, dog food was spilled on the floor, a broken glass lay under the table, and a small pile of sand was spread by the back door.

He quickly headed up the stairs, stepping over toys and more piles of clothes, looking for his wife. He was worried she may be ill, or that something serious had happened. He found her lounging in the bedroom, still curled in the bed in her pajamas, reading a novel. She looked up at him, smiled, and asked how his day went.

He looked at her bewildered and asked, "What happened here today?"

She smiled again and answered, "You know every day when you come home from work and ask me what in the world I did today?"

"Yes." was his incredulous reply.

She answered, "Well, today I didn't do it."

Bubba's Friends

Bubba was bragging to his boss one day, "You know, I know everyone there is to know. Just name someone, anyone, and I know them."

Tired of his boasting, his boss called his bluff, "OK, Bubba how about Tom Cruise?"

"Sure, yes, Tom and I are old friends, and I can prove it."

So Bubba and his boss fly out to Hollywood and knock on Tom Cruise's door, and sure enough, Tom Cruise, shouts, "Bubba! Great to see you! You and your friend come right in and join me for lunch!"

Although impressed, Bubba's boss is still skeptical. After they leave Cruise's house, he tells Bubba that he thinks Bubba's knowing Cruise was just lucky.

"No, no, just name anyone else," Bubba says.

"President Bush." his boss quickly retorts.

"Yes," Bubba says, "I know him, let's fly out to Washington."

And off they go. At the White House, Bush spots Bubba on the tour and motions him and his boss over, saying, "Bubba, what a surprise. I was just on my way to a meeting, but you and your friend come on in and let's have a cup of coffee first and catch up."

Well, the boss is very shaken by now, but still not totally convinced. After they leave the White house grounds, he expresses his doubts to Bubba, who again implores him to name anyone else.

"The Pope," his boss replies.

"Sure!" says Bubba. "My folks are from Poland, and I've known the Pope a long time."

So off they fly to Rome. Bubba and his boss are assembled with the masses in Vatican Square when Bubba says, "This will never work. I can't catch the Pope's eye among all these people. Tell you what, I know all the guards so let me just go upstairs and I'll come out on the balcony with the Pope."

And he disappears into the crowd headed toward the Vatican. Sure enough, half an hour later Bubba emerges with the Pope on the balcony.

But by the time Bubba returns, he finds that his boss has had a heart attack and is surrounded by paramedics. Working his way to his boss' side, Bubba asks him, "What happened?"

His boss looks up and says, "I was doing fine until you and the Pope came out on the balcony and the man next to me said, 'Who's that on the balcony with Bubba?'"

$100.00 Please

A little boy, who wanted $100.00 very badly, prayed for two weeks but nothing happened. Then he decided to write GOD a letter requesting $100.00.

When the postal authorities received the letter addressed to GOD, U.S.A., they decided to send it to the President. The President was so impressed, touched, and amused that he instructed his secretary to send the boy $5.00. Mr. President thought that this would appear to be a lot of money to the little boy.

The little boy was delighted with the $5.00 and immediately sat down to write a thank you note to GOD that read: "Dear God, Thank you very much for sending me the money.

However, I noticed that for some reason you had to send it through Washington, D.C., and, as usual, they deducted $95.00."

"Not" Working

Dear Secretary of Agriculture,

My friends, Darryl and Janice, over at Jonestown, Oklahoma, received a check the other day for $1,000 from the government for not raising hogs. So, I want to go into the "not raising hogs" business myself next year.

What I want to know is, in your opinion, what is the best type of farm not to raise hogs on, and what is the best breed of hogs not to raise? I want to be sure that I approach this endeavor in keeping with all government policies. I would prefer not to raise Razor hogs, but if that is not a good breed not to raise, then I can just as easily not raise Yorkshires or Durocs.

As I see it, the hardest part of this program will be keeping an accurate inventory of how many hogs I haven't raised. If I can get $1,000 for not raising 50 hogs, will I get $2,000 for not raising 100 hogs? I plan to operate on a small scale at first, holding myself down to about 4,000 "not raised" hogs, which will give me $80,000 income the first year. Then I can buy an airplane.

Now another thing: these hogs I will not raise will not eat 100,000 bushels of corn. I understand that you also pay farmers for not raising corn and wheat. Will I qualify for payments for not raising wheat and corn not to feed the 4,000 hogs I am not going to raise? I want to get started not feeding as soon as possible, as this seems to be a good time of the year to not raise hogs and grain.

I am also considering the "not milking cows" business, so please send me any information on that also.

In view of these circumstances, I understand that the government will consider me totally unemployed, so I plan to file for unemployment and food stamps as well.

Be assured that you will have my vote in the coming elections.

Patriotically yours,

Duster Benton

Kids on Marriage

How Does a Person Decide Who to Marry?

"You flip a nickel, and heads means you stay with him and tails means you try the next one." Kally, age 9

"You got to find somebody who likes the same stuff. Like if you like sports, she should like it that you like sports, and she should keep the chips and dip coming." Allan, age 10

"No person really decides before they grow up who they're going to marry. God decides it all way before, and you got to find out later who you're stuck with." Kirsten, age 10

Concerning the Proper Age to Get Married

"Twenty-three is the best age because you know the person FOREVER by then!" Cam, age 10

"No age is good to get married at.... You got to be a fool to get married!" Freddie, age 6

How Can a Stranger Tell if Two People are Married?

"Married people usually look happy to talk to other people." Eddie, age 6

"You might have to guess based on whether they seem to be yelling at the same kids." Derrick, age 8

What Do You Think Your Mom and Dad Have in Common?

"Both don't want no more kids." Lori, age 8

What Do Most People Do on a Date?

"Dates are for having fun, and people should use them to get to know each other. Even boys have something to say if you listen long enough." Lynnette, age 8

"On the first date, they just tell each other lies, and that usually gets them interested enough to go for a second date." Martin, age 10

103

What the Children Would Do on a First Date That Was Turning Sour

"I'd run home and play dead. The next day I would call all the newspapers and make sure they wrote about me in all the dead columns." Craig, age 9

When is It Okay to Kiss Someone?

"When they're rich!" Pam, age 7

"The law says you have to be eighteen, so I wouldn't want to mess with that." Curt, age 7

"The rule goes like this: If you kiss someone, then you should marry them and have kids with them... It's the right thing to do." Howard, age 8

The Great Debate: Is It Better to Be Single or Married?

"It's better for girls to be single but not for boys. Boys need somebody to clean up after them!" Anita, age 9

"Single is better ... for the simple reason that I wouldn't want to change no diapers... Of course, if I did get married, I'd figure something out. I'd just phone my mother and have her come over for some coffee and diaper-changing." Kirsten, age 10

What Advice Do You Have for a Young Couple About to Be Married?

"The first thing I'd say to them is: 'Listen up, youngins ... I got something to say to you. Why in the heck do you wanna get married, anyway?'" Craig, age 9

What Promises Do a Man and a Woman Make When They Get Married?

"A man and a woman promise to go through sickness and illness and diseases together." Marlon, age 10

How to Make a Marriage Work

"Tell your wife that she looks pretty even if she looks like a truck." Ricky, age 7

How Would the World Be Different if People Didn't Get Married?

"There sure would be a lot of kids to explain, wouldn't there?" Kelvin, age 8

"You can be sure of one thing - the boys would come chasing after us just the same as they do now!" Roberta, age 7

Cheap Perfume

After being away on business, Tom thought it would be nice to bring his wife a little gift. "How about some perfume?" he asked the cosmetics clerk.

She showed him a bottle costing $50.00. "That's a bit much," said Tom, so she returned with a smaller bottle for $30.00.

"That's still quite a bit," Tom groused.

Growing annoyed, the clerk brought out a tiny $15.00 bottle.

"What I mean," said Tom, "is I'd like to see something really cheap."

So the clerk handed him a mirror.

How You Can Tell It's Going to Be a Rotten Day

You wake up face down on the pavement.

You call Suicide Prevention and they put you on hold.

You see a "60 Minutes" news team waiting in your office.

Your birthday cake collapses from the weight of the candles.

Your twin sister forgot your birthday.

You wake up and discover your waterbed broke and then realize you don't have a waterbed.

Your car horn goes off accidentally and remains stuck as you follow a group of Hell's Angels on the freeway.

Your wife wakes up feeling amorous and you have a headache.

Your boss tells you not to bother to take off your coat.

You wake up and your braces are locked together.

You walk to work and find your dress is stuck in the back of your pantyhose.

You call your answering service and they tell you it's none of your business.

Your income tax check bounces.

You put both contact lenses in the same eye.

The bird singing outside your window is a buzzard.

Letter from Goober Mother to her Goober Son

Dear Son,

I am writing slow because I know you can't read fast. We don't live where we did when you left. Your Dad read in the paper that most accidents happen within 20 miles of home, so we moved. I won't be able to send you the address, because the last family that lived here took the house numbers with them so they would not have to change their address.

This place has a washing machine. The first day I put four shirts in it, pulled down on the handle and haven't seen them since. It rained twice this week, three days the first time and four days the second time.

Aunt Sue said the coat you wanted me to send you, would be a little too heavy to send in the mail with all them heavy buttons, so we cut them off and put them in the pocket for you.

The family is fine. Your Father, he has a lovely job. He has about 500 men under him. He is cutting grass down at the cemetery. Your sister had a baby this morning. I haven't found out yet whether it's a girl or a boy so I don't know if you are an aunt or an uncle. We got a bill from the funeral home the other day. They said if we didn't make the last payment on Grandma's funeral bill, up she comes.

Three of your friends went off the bridge in a pick-up. Billy Bob was driving and Willie and Joe was in the back. Billy Bob got out, he rolled down the window and swam to safety. The other two drowned, they couldn't get the tailgate down.

Your Uncle John fell in a whisky vat. Some men tried to pull him out but he fought them off before he drowned. We cremated him and he burned for three days.

Not much more news this time. Nothin' much happened.

Write more often.

Love, Mom   P.S. I was going to send you some money but the envelope was already sealed.

Progressive Motherhood

Yes, parenthood changes everything. But parenthood also changes with each baby. Here are some of the ways having a second and third child differs from having your first:

YOUR CLOTHES

1st baby: You begin wearing maternity clothes as soon as your OB/GYN confirms your pregnancy.

2nd baby: You wear your regular clothes for as long as possible.

3rd baby: Your maternity clothes are your regular clothes.

THE BABY'S NAME

1st baby: You pore over baby-name books and practice pronouncing and writing combinations of all your favorites.

2nd baby: Someone has to name their kid after your great-aunt Mavis, right? It might as well be you.

3rd baby: You open a name book, close your eyes, and see where your finger falls. Bimaldo? Perfect!

PREPARING FOR THE BIRTH

1st baby: You practice your breathing religiously.

2nd baby: You don't bother practicing because you remember that last time, breathing didn't do a thing.

3rd baby: You ask for an epidural in your 8th month.

THE LAYETTE

1st baby: You pre-wash your new-born's clothes, color-coordinate them, and fold them neatly in the baby's little bureau.

2nd baby: You check to make sure that the clothes are clean and discard only the ones with the darkest stains.

3rd baby: Boys can wear pink, can't they?

WORRIES

1st baby: At the first sign of distress - a whimper, a frown - you pick up the baby.

2nd baby: You pick the baby up when her wails threaten to wake your firstborn.

3rd baby: You teach your 3-year-old how to rewind the mechanical swing.

ACTIVITIES

1st baby: You take your infant to Baby Gymnastics, Baby Swing, and Baby Story Hour.

2nd baby: You take your infant to Baby Gymnastics.

3rd baby: You take your infant to the supermarket and the dry cleaner.

GOING OUT

1st baby: The first time you leave your baby with a sitter, you call home 5 times.

2nd baby: Just before you walk out the door, you remember to leave a number where you can be reached.

3rd baby: You leave instructions for the sitter to call only if she sees blood.

AT HOME

1st baby: You spend a good bit of every day just gazing at the baby.

2nd baby: You spend a bit of every day watching to be sure your older child isn't squeezing, poking, or hitting the baby.

3rd baby: You spend a little bit of every day hiding from the children.

Boy Scout Survival Tips

A Scout Master was teaching his boy scouts about survival in the desert.

"What are the three most important things you should bring with you in case you get lost in the desert?" he asked. Several hands went up, and many important things were suggested such as food, matches, etc.

Then one little boy in the back eagerly raised his hand. "Yes Timmy, what are the three most important things you would bring with you?" asked the Scout Master.

Timmy replied, "A compass, a canteen of water, and a deck of cards."

"Why is that, Timmy?"

"Well," answered Timmy, "the compass is to find the right direction, the water is to prevent dehydration..."

"And what about the deck of cards?" asked the Scout Master impatiently.

"Well, Sir, as soon as you start playing Solitaire, someone is bound to come up behind you and say, "Put that red nine on top of that black ten!"

12 Things Not To Say When Pulled Over By A Cop:

I can't reach my license unless you hold my beer.

Sorry, Officer, I didn't realize my radar detector wasn't plugged in.

Aren't you the guy from the Village People?

Hey, you must've been doin' 125 mph to keep up with me. Good job!

Are you Andy or Barney?

I thought you had to be in relatively good physical condition to be a police officer.

You're not gonna check the trunk are you?

I pay your salary!

Gee, Officer! That's terrific. The last officer only gave me a warning too!

Do you know why you pulled me over? Okay, just so one of us does.

I was trying to keep up with traffic. Yes, I know there are no other cars around. That's how far ahead of me they are.

When the Officer says "Gee Son...Your eyes look red, have you been drinking?" You probably shouldn't respond with, "Gee Officer, your eyes looked glazed, have you been eating donuts?"

Soap and Water

A minister was asked to dinner by one of his parishioners, whom he knew was an unkempt housekeeper.

When he sat down at the table, he noticed that the dishes were the dirtiest that he had ever seen in his life.

"Were these dishes ever washed?" he asked his hostess, running his fingers over the grit and grime.

She replied, "They're as clean as soap and water could get them."

He felt a bit apprehensive, but blessed the food anyway and started eating. It was really delicious and he said so, despite the dirty dishes.

When dinner was over, the hostess took the dishes outside and yelled, "Here Soap! Here Water!"

Politically Correct Football
(www.nfl.com can help you figuring this one out)

The Politically Correct National Football League would like to announce its name changes and schedules for the '99 season:

The Washington Native Americans will host the New York Very Tall People on opening day.

Other key games include the Dallas Western-Style Laborers hosting the St. Louis Uninvited Guests, and the Minnesota Plundering Norsemen taking on the Green Bay Meat Industry Workers.

In Week 2, there are several key match-ups, highlighted by the showdown between the San Francisco Precious Metal Enthusiasts and the New Orleans Pretty Good People. The Atlanta Birds of Prey will play host to the Philadelphia Birds of Prey, while the Seattle Birds of Prey will visit the Phoenix Male Finches.

The Monday night game will pit the Miami Pelagic Percoid Food Fishes against the Denver Untamed Beasts of Burden.

The Cincinnati Large Bangladeshi Carnivorous Mammals will travel to Tampa Bay for a clash with the West Indies Freebooters later in Week 9, and the Detroit Large Carnivorous Cats will play the Chicago Securities-Traders-in-a-Declining-Market. Week 9 also features the Indianapolis Young Male Horses at the New England Zealous Lovers of Country.

A Goober Wins!

A goober goes to a restaurant, buys a coffee and sits down to drink it. He looks on the side of his cup and finds a peal off prize. He pulls off the tab and yells, "I WON! I WON! I WON a motor home, I WON a motor home!"

The waitress runs over and says, "That's impossible. The biggest prize given away was a mini van!" The goober replies, "No, I WON a motor home, I WON a motor home!"

By this time the manager makes his way over to the table and says, "You couldn't possibly have won a motor home because we didn't have that as a prize!" Again the goober says, "No, no mistake, I WON a motor home, I WON a motor home!"

The goober hands the prize ticket to the manager and he reads, "WIN A BAGEL."

You know it's time to turn your computer off and read a book when .....

- A friend calls and says, "How are you? Your phones have been busy for a year!!!!"

- You forgot how to work the TV remote control.

- You see something funny and scream, "LOL, LOL."

- You meet the mailman at the curb and you are sure he said YOU'VE GOT MAIL.

- You sign off and your screen says you were on for 3 days and 45 minutes.

- You fall asleep, but instead of dreams you get IMs.

- You buy a laptop and a cell phone so you can have AOL in your car.

- Tech support calls YOU for help.

- You beg your friends to get an account so you can "hang out."

- You get a second phone line just to call out for pizza.

- You purchase a vanity car license plate with your screen name on it. (never thought of that.....BUT)

- You say "he he he he" or "heh heh heh" instead of laughing.

- You say "SCROLL UP" when someone asks what it was you said.

- You sneak away to your computer when everyone goes to sleep.

- You talk on the phone with the same person you are sending an instant message to.

- You look at an annoying person off line and wish that you had your ignore button handy.

- You start to experience "withdrawal" after not being online for a while.

- You sit on AOL for 6 hours waiting for that certain special person to sign on.

- You get up in the morning and go online before getting your coffee.

- .....You end your sentences with.....three or more periods.......

- You've gone to an unstaffed AOL room to give tech support.

- You think faster than the computer.

- You enter a room and get greeted by 25 people with {{{hugs}}} and**kisses**.

- Being called a "newbie" is a major insult to you.

- You're on the phone and say BRB.

- Your teacher, spouse, or boss recommends a drug test for the blood shot eyes.

- Your answering machine/voice mail sounds a little like this.... "BRB. Leave your S/N and I'll TTYL ASAP".

- You need to be pried from your computer by the Jaws-of-life.

- The same jokes you sent to one friend come back in five minutes from a mutual friend that you forgot to put on distribution.

Signs

In the front yard of a funeral home: "Drive carefully, we'll wait."

On an electrician's truck: "Let us remove your shorts."

In a nonsmoking area: "If we see you smoking, we will assume you are on fire and take appropriate action."

On a maternity room door: "Push, Push, Push."

On a front door: "Everyone on the premises is a vegetarian except the dog."

At an optometrist's office: "If you don't see what you're looking for, you've come to the right place."

On a taxidermist's window: "We really know our stuff."

On a butcher's window: "Let me meat your needs."

On a fence: "Salesmen welcome. Dog food is expensive."

At a car dealership: "The best way to get back on your feet -- miss a car payment."

Outside a muffler shop: "No appointment necessary. We'll hear you coming."

On a desk in a reception room: "We shoot every 3rd salesman, and the 2nd one just left."

In a veterinarian's waiting room: "Be back in 5 minutes. Sit! Stay!"

At the electric company: "We would be delighted if you send in your bill. However, if you don't, you will be."

In a Beauty Shop: "Dye now!"

On the side of a garbage truck: "We've got what it takes to take what you've got."

In a restaurant window: "Don't stand there and be hungry, come in and get fed up."

Inside a bowling alley: "Please be quiet. We need to hear a pin drop."

In a cafeteria: "Shoes are required to eat in the cafeteria. Socks can eat any place they want."

Religious Lady on the Plane

There was a religious lady that had to do a lot of traveling for her business, so naturally she did a lot of flying. Flying made her extremely nervous, so she always took her Bible along with her to read since it helped relax her on the long flights.

One time, she was sitting next to a man. When he saw her pull out her Bible, he gave a little chuckle, smirked and went back to what he was doing. After a while, he turned to her and asked, "You don't really believe all that stuff in there do you?"

The lady replied, "Of course I do. It is the Bible."

He said, "Well, what about the guy that was swallowed by the whale?"

She replied, "Oh, Jonah. Yes, I believe that, it is in the Bible."

He asked, "Well, how do you suppose he survived all that time?"

The lady said, "Well, I don't really know. I guess when I get to heaven, I will ask him."

"What if he isn't in heaven?" the man asked sarcastically.

"Then you can ask him," replied the lady.

One Liners

43.3% of statistics are meaningless!

Circular Definition: see Definition, Circular.

A.A.A.A.: An organization for drunks who drive.

It said 'Insert disk #3', but only two will fit.

Which is the non-smoking lifeboat?

I I I I I I I ////// __ __ __ __ __ The domino effect at work.

Originality is the art of concealing your sources.

Just fill out one simple form to win a Tax Audit!

Democracy: Four wolves and a lamb voting on lunch.

113

The buck doesn't even slow down here!

Don't assume malice for what stupidity can explain.

If you think talk is cheap, try hiring a lawyer.

Oh, no! Not ANOTHER learning experience!

The only cure for insomnia is to get more sleep.

Advice is free: The right answer will cost plenty.

Don't insult the alligator until after you cross the river.

Nothing's impossible for those who don't have to do it.

Two can live as cheaply as one, for half as long.

My life has a superb cast, but I can't figure out the plot.

'Oh what a tangled web we weave' - Hair Club for Men.

A penny saved is a government oversight.

Shin: Device for finding furniture in the dark.

Laughing stock: cattle with a sense of humor.

Wood Cutter

This fellow is looking to buy a saw to cut down some trees in his back yard. He goes to a chainsaw shop and asks about various chainsaws. The dealer tells him, "Look, I have a lot of models, but why don't you save yourself a lot of time and aggravation and get the top-of-the-line model. This chainsaw will cut a hundred cords of wood for you per day."

So, the man takes the chainsaw home and begins working on the trees. After cutting for several hours and only cutting two cords, he decides to quit. He thinks there is something wrong with the chainsaw. "How can I cut for hours and only cut two cords?" the man asks himself. "Tomorrow, I will begin first thing in the morning and cut all day," the man tells himself. So, the next morning the man gets up at 4 a.m. and cuts and cuts and cuts till nightfall, and still he only manages to cut five cords.

The man is convinced this is a bad saw. "The dealer told me it would cut one hundred cords of wood in a day, no problem. I will take this saw back to the dealer," the man says to himself.

The very next day the man brings the saw back to the dealer and explains the problem. The dealer, baffled by the man's claim, removes the chainsaw from the case. He says, "Hmm, it looks OK."

Then the dealer starts the chainsaw, to which the man responds, "What's that noise?"

Euro-English

The European Commission has just announced an agreement whereby English will be the official language of the European Union rather than German, which was the other possibility.

As part of the negotiations Her Majesty's Government conceded that English spelling had some room for improvement and has accepted a 5-year phase-in plan that would be known as "Euro-English".

In the first year, 's' will replace the soft 'c'. Sertainly, this will make the sivil servants jump with joy. The hard 'c' will be dropped in favour of the 'k'. This should klear up konfusion and keyboards kan have one less letter.

There will be growing publik enthusiasm in the sekond year when the troublesome 'ph' will be replased with the 'f'. This will make words like 'fotograf' 20% shorter.

In the third year, publik akseptanse of the new spelling kan be expekted to reach the stage where more komplikated changes are possible. Governments will enkourage the removal of double leters which have always been a deterent to akurate speling. Also al wil agre that the horibl mes of the silent 'e' in the languag is disgrasful and it should go away.

By the 4th yer peopl wil be reseptiv to steps such as replasing 'th' with 'z' and 'w' with 'v'. During ze fifz yer, ze unesesary 'o' kan be dropd from vords kontaining 'ou' and similar changes vud of kors be aplid to oza kombinations of letas.

After ziz fifz yer ve vil have a rali sensibl riten styl. Zer vil be no mor trubl or difikultis and evrivun vil find it ezi tu anderstand ech oza. Ze drem of an united Urop vil finali kum tru!

Reading at Lunchtime

A Jewish man took his Passover lunch to eat outside in the park. He sat down on a bench and began eating. Since Jews do not eat leavened bread during the eight-day holiday, he was eating Matzo, a flat crunchy unleavened bread that has dozens of perforations.

A little while later a blind man came by and sat down next to him. Feeling neighborly, the Jewish man passed a sheet of matzo to the blind man.

The blind man handled the matzo on both sides for a few minutes, looked puzzled, and finally exclaimed, "Who wrote this junk?"

115

Surprise Company? 30 Minutes to a Cleaner House

Welcome, ladies and gentlemen, to the first session of Housekeeping Tips for Regular People. If you're a Martha Stewart type of housekeeper, this is NOT for you. However, for the rest of you, this is your chance to learn 15 Secret Shortcuts to Good Housekeeping that your mother never told you.

SECRET TIP 1: DOOR LOCKS

If a room clearly can't be whipped into shape in 30 seconds, much less 30 minutes, employ the Locked Door Method of cleaning. Tell anyone who tries to go in the room that the door is intentionally locked. CAUTION: It is not advisable to use this tip for the bathroom.

Time: 2 seconds

SECRET TIP 2: DUCT TAPE

No home should be without an ample supply. Not only is it handy for plumbing repairs, but it's also a great way to hem drapes, tablecloths, clothes, just about anything. No muss, no fuss.

Time: 2-3 minutes

SECRET TIP 3: OVENS

If you think ovens are just for baking, think again. Ovens represent at least 9 cubic feet of hidden storage space, which means they're a great place to shove dirty dishes, dirty clothes, or just about anything you want to get out of sight when company's coming.

Time: 2 minutes

SECRET TIP 4: CLOTHES DRYERS

Like Secret Tip 3, except bigger. CAUTION: Avoid hiding flammable objects here.

Time: 2.5 minutes

SECRET TIP 5: WASHING MACHINES & FREEZERS

Like Secret Tip 4, except even bigger.

Time: 3 minutes

SECRET TIP 6: DUST RUFFLES

No bed should be without one. Devotees of Martha Stewart believe dust ruffles exist to keep dust out from under a bed or to help coordinate the colorful look of a bedroom. The rest of us know a dust ruffle's highest and best use is to hide whatever you've managed to shove under the bed. (Refer to Tips 3, 4 & 5)

Time: 4 minutes

SECRET TIP 7: DUSTING

The 30-Minutes-To-A-Clean-House method says: Never dust under what you can dust around.

Time: 3 minutes

SECRET TIP 8: DISHES

Don't use them. Use plastic or paper and you won't have to do any.
Time: 1 minute

SECRET TIP 9: CLOTHES WASHING (EEWWW)

This secret tip is brought to you by an inventive teenager. When this teen's mother went on a housekeeping strike for a month, the teen discovered you can extend the life of your underwear by two ...if you turn it wrong side out and, yes, re-wear it. CAUTION: This tip is recommended only for teens and those who don't care if they get in a car wreck.

Time: 3 seconds

SECRET TIP 10: IRONING

If an article of clothing doesn't require a full press and your hair does, a curling iron is the answer. In between curling your hair, use the hot wand to iron minor wrinkles out of your clothes. Yes, it really does work, or so I'm told, by other disciples of the 30-Minutes-To-A-Clean-House philosophy.

Time: 5 minutes (including curling your hair)

SECRET TIP 11: VACUUMING

Stick to the middle of the room, which is the only place people look. Don't bother vacuuming under furniture. It takes way too long and no one looks there anyway.

Time: entire house, 5 minutes; living room only, 2 minutes.

SECRET TIP 12: LIGHTING

The key here is low, low, and lower. It's not only romantic, but bad lighting can hide a multitude of dirt.

Time: 10 seconds

SECRET TIP 13: BED MAKING

Get an old-fashioned waterbed. No one can tell if those things are made up or not, saving you, oh, hundreds of seconds over the course of a lifetime.

Time: 0 minutes

SECRET TIP 14: SHOWERS, TOILETS, AND SINKS

Forget one and two. Concentrate on three.

Time: 1 minute

SECRET TIP 15:

If you already knew at least 10 of these tips, don't even think about inviting a Martha Stewart type to your home.

Talking Clock

While proudly showing off his new apartment to friends, a college student led the way into the den.

"What is the big brass gong and hammer for?" one of his friends asked.

"That is the talking clock," the man replied.

"How's it work?" the friend asked.

"Watch," the man said then proceeded to give the gong an ear shattering pound with the hammer. BONG!

Suddenly someone screamed from the other side of the wall "KNOCK IT OFF, YOU GOOBER! IT'S TWO A.M.!"

Reasons Not to Wash

If you took the same excuses that people use for not going to church and apply them to other important areas of life you'd realize how inconsistent we can be in our logic. For example: "Reasons Not To Wash."

1. I was forced to as a child.

2. People who make soap are only after your money.

3. I wash on special occasions like Christmas and Easter.

4. People who wash are hypocrites; they think they are cleaner than everyone else.

5. There are so many different kinds of soap, I can't decide which one is best.

6. I used to wash, but it got boring so I stopped.

7. None of my friends wash.

8. The bathroom is never warm enough in the winter or cool enough in the summer.

9. I'll start washing when I get older and dirtier.

10. I can't spare the time.

Just A Kiss Per Yard

Walking up to a department store's fabric counter, a pretty girl asked, "I want to buy this material for a new dress. How much does it cost?"

"Only one kiss per yard," replied the smirking male clerk. "That's fine," replied the girl. "I'll take ten yards."

With expectation and anticipation written all over his face, the clerk quickly measured out and wrapped the cloth, then teasingly held it out.

The girl snapped up the package and pointed to a little old man standing beside her.

"Grandpa will pay the bill," she smiled.

New Boater

This past summer, down on Lake Isabella, located in the high desert, an hour east of Bakersfield, a fellow new to boating was having a problem.

No matter how hard he tried, he just couldn't get his brand new 22-ft Bayliner to perform. It wouldn't get on a plane at all, and was very sluggish in almost every maneuver, no matter how much power he supplied. After about an hour of trying to make it go, he putted over to a nearby marina. Maybe they could tell him what was wrong.

A thorough topside check revealed everything was in perfect working order. The engine ran fine, the outdrive went up and down, the prop was the correct size and pitch. So, one of the marina guys jumped in the water to check underneath. He came up choking on water he was laughing so hard. Under the boat, still strapped securely in place, was the trailer.

Bangety Bang Bang

Seems there was a young soldier, who, just before battle, told his sergeant that he didn't have a rifle.

"That's no problem, son," said the sergeant. "Here, take this broom. Just point it at the enemy, and go 'Bangety Bang Bang'."

"But what about a bayonet, Sarge?" asked the young (and gullible) recruit.

The sergeant pulls a piece of straw from the end of the broom, and attaches it to the handle end. "Here, use this... just go, 'Stabbity Stab Stab'".

The recruit ends up alone on the battlefield, holding just his broom. Suddenly, an enemy soldier charges at him. The recruit points the broom.

"Bangety Bang Bang!" The enemy falls dead.

More enemies appear. The recruit, amazed at his good luck, goes "Bangety Bang Bang! Stabbity Stab Stab!" He mows down the enemy by the dozens. Finally, the battlefield is clear, except for one enemy soldier walking slowly toward him.

"Bangety Bang Bang!" shouts the recruit. The enemy keeps coming. "Bangety Bang Bang!" repeats the recruit, to no avail. He gets desperate. "Bangety Bang Bang! Stabbity Stab Stab!" It's no use.

The enemy keeps coming. He stomps the recruit into the ground, and says... "Tankety Tank Tank."

More Sayings

- Blessed are those who hunger and thirst, for they are sticking to their diets.

- Life is an endless struggle full of frustrations and challenges, but eventually you find a hairstylist you like.

- You're getting old when you get the same sensation from a rocking chair that you once got from a roller coaster.

- One of life's mysteries is how a two pound box of candy can make a person gain five pounds.

- It's frustrating when you know all the answers, but nobody bothers to ask you the questions.

- If you can remain calm, you just don't have all the facts.

- I finally got my head together, and my body fell apart.

- Time may be a great healer, but it's also a lousy beautician.

- Brain cells come and brain cells go, but fat cells live forever.

- Age doesn't always bring wisdom. Sometimes age comes alone.

- Life not only begins at forty; it begins to show.

- Just when I was getting used to yesterday, along came today.

- Sometimes I think I understand everything, then I regain consciousness.

- If at first you don't succeed, see if the loser gets anything.

- You don't stop laughing because you grow old; you grow old because you stop laughing.

- I don't mind the rat race, but I could do with a little more cheese.

- Amazing! You just hang something in your closet for a while, and it shrinks two sizes.

- It is bad to suppress laughter; it goes back down and spreads to your hips.

- Age is important only if you're cheese or wine.

- The only time a woman wishes she were a year older is when she is expecting a baby.

- Freedom of the press means no-iron clothes.

- Inside some of us is a thin person struggling to get out, but they can usually be sedated with a few pieces of chocolate cake.

- Can it be a mistake that "STRESSED" is "DESSERTS" spelled backwards?

- Seen it all, done it all, can't remember most of it.

- Despite the high cost of living, have you noticed how it remains so popular?

Something Nice For Dad

Unable to attend the funeral after his father died, a son who lived far away called his brother and told him, "Do something nice for Dad and send me the bill."

Later, he got a bill for $200.00, which he paid. The next month, he got another bill for $200.00, which he also paid, figuring it was some incidental expense.

Bills for $200.00 kept arriving every month, and finally the man called his brother again to find out what was going on.

"Well," said the other brother, "you said to do something nice for Dad. So I rented him a tuxedo."

Miscellaneous Goobers

GOOBERS AT WORK:

I was signing the receipt for my credit card purchase when the clerk noticed that I had never signed my name on the back of the credit card. She informed me that she could not complete the transaction unless the card was signed. When I asked why, she explained that it was necessary to compare the signature on the credit card with the signature I just signed on the receipt. So I signed the credit card in front of her. She carefully compared that signature to the one I signed on the receipt. As luck would have it, they matched.

GOOBERS & GEOGRAPHY:

After interviewing a particularly short-spoken job candidate, I described the person to my boss as rather monosyllabic. My boss said, "Really? Where is Monosyllabia?" Thinking that he was just kidding, I played along and said that it was just south of Elbonia. He replied, "Oh, you mean over by Croatia?"

ADVICE FOR GOOBERS:

An actual tip from page 16 of the HP Environmental, Health & Safety Handbook for Employees: "Blink your eyelids periodically to lubricate your eyes."

GOOBERS IN THE NEIGHBORHOOD:

I live in a semi-rural area. We recently had a new neighbor call the local township administrative office to request the removal of the Deer Crossing sign on our road. The reason: Many deer were being hit by cars and he no longer wanted them to cross there.

GOOBERS & COMPUTERS:

My neighbor works in the operations department in the central office of a large bank. Employees in the field call him when they have problems with their computers. One night he got a call from a woman in one of the branch banks who had this question: "I've got smoke coming from the back of my terminal. Do you guys have a fire downtown?"

GOOBERS ARE EASY TO PLEASE:

I was sitting in my science class, when the teacher commented that the next day would be the shortest day of the year. My lab partner became visibly excited, cheering and clapping. I explained to her that the amount of daylight changes, not the actual amount of time. Needless to say, she was very disappointed.

GOOBERS IN FOOD SERVICE:

My daughter went to a local Taco Bell and ordered a taco. She asked the individual behind the counter for "minimal lettuce." He said he was sorry, but they only had iceberg.

A GOOBER'S GOOBER:

Police in Radnor, Pennsylvania, interrogated a suspect by placing a metal colander on his head and connecting it with wires to a photocopy machine. The message "He's lying" was placed in the copier, and police pressed the copy button each time they thought the suspect was telling a lie. Believing the "lie detector" was working, the suspect confessed.

A Father's Method

A loaded mini van pulled in to the only remaining campsite. Four children leapt from the vehicle and began feverishly unloading gear and setting up the tent. The boys rushed to gather firewood, while the girls and their mother set up the camp stove and cooking utensils.

A nearby camper marveled to the youngsters' father, "That, sir, is some display of teamwork."

The father replied, "I have a system; no one goes to the bathroom until the camp is set up."

Thoughts on Growing Old

- Maybe it's true that life begins at fifty. But everything else starts to wear out, fall out, or spread out.

- There are three signs of old age. The first is your loss of memory. I forget the other two.

- You're getting old when you don't care where your spouse goes, just as long as you don't have to go along.

- Middle age is when work is a lot less fun--and fun is a lot more work.

- Statistics show that at the age of seventy, there are five women to every man. Isn't that the worst time for a guy to get those odds?

- You know you're getting on in years when the girls at the office start confiding in you.

- Middle age is when it takes longer to rest than to get tired.

- By the time a man is wise enough to watch his step, he's too old to go anywhere.

- Middle age is when you have stopped growing at both ends, and have begun to grow in the middle.

- A man has reached middle age when he is cautioned to slow down by his doctor instead of by the police.

- You know you're into middle age when you realize that caution is the only thing you care to exercise.

- Don't worry about avoiding temptation. As you grow older, it will avoid you.

- The aging process could be slowed down if it had to work its way through Congress.

- You know you're getting old when you're sitting in a rocker and you can't get it started.

- You know you're getting old when you wake up with that morning-after feeling, and you didn't do anything the night before.

- The cardiologist's diet: if it tastes good, spit it out.

- Doctor to patient: I have good news and bad news. The good news is that you are not a hypochondriac.

- It's hard to be nostalgic when you can't remember anything.

- You know you're getting old when you stop buying green bananas.

- Last Will and Testament: Being of sound mind, I spent all my money.

- When you lean over to pick something up off the floor, you ask yourself if there is anything else you need to do while you are down there.

- You find yourself in the middle of the stairway, and you can't remember if you were downstairs going up or upstairs going down.

Pessimistic Friend

An avid duck hunter was in the market for a new bird dog. His search ended when he found a dog that could actually walk on water to retrieve a duck.

Shocked by his find, he was sure none of his friends would ever believe him. He decided to try to break the news to a friend of his, a pessimist by nature, and invited him to hunt with him and his new dog. As they waited by the shore, a flock of ducks flew by. They fired and a duck fell. The dog responded and jumped into the water. The dog, however, did not sink but instead walked across the water to retrieve the bird, never getting more than his paws wet. The friend saw everything but did not say a single word.

On the drive home the hunter asked his friend, "Did you notice anything unusual about my new dog?"

"I sure did," responded his friend. "He can't swim."

Why Parents Get Gray

The boss of a big company needed to call one of his employees about an urgent problem with one of the main computers. He dialed the employees home phone number and was greeted with a child's whispered, "Hello?"

Feeling put out at the inconvenience of having to talk to a youngster the boss asked, "Is your Daddy home?"

"Yes," whispered the small voice.

"May I talk with him?" the man asked.

To the surprise of the boss, the small voice whispered, "No."

Wanting to talk with an adult, the boss asked, "Is your Mommy there?"

"Yes," came the answer.

"May I talk with her?"

Again the small voice whispered, "No."

Knowing that it was not likely that a young child would be left home alone, the boss decided he would just leave a message with the person who should be there watching over the child. "Is there any one there besides you?" the boss asked the child.

"Yes," whispered the child. "A policeman."

125

Wondering what a cop would be doing at his employee's home, the boss asked, "May I speak with the policeman?"

"No, he's busy," whispered the child.

"Busy doing what?" asked the boss.

"Talking to Daddy and Mommy and the Fireman," came the quiet reply.

Growing concerned and even worried as he heard what sounded like a helicopter through the earpiece on the phone the boss asked, "What is that noise?"

"A hello-copper," answered the whispering voice.

"What is going on there?" asked the boss, now alarmed.

In an awed whispering voice the child answered, "The search team just landed the hello-copper."

Alarmed, concerned and more than just a little frustrated the boss asked, "Why are they there?"

Still whispering, the young voice replied along with a muffled giggle, "They're looking for me."

Understanding the Metric System

1 million microphones = 1 megaphone

1 million bicycles = 2 megacycles

2000 mockingbirds = 2 kilomockingbirds

10 cards = 1 decacards (or is it 52 cards = 1 deck-a-cards?)

1/2 lavatory = 1 demijohn

1 millionth of a fish = 1 microfiche

453.6 graham crackers = 1 pound cake

10 rations = 1 decoration

10 millipedes = 1 centipede

3-1/3 tridents = 1 decadent

10 monologs = 5 dialogues

2 monograms = 1 diagram

8 nickels = 2 paradigms

Top Ten Things You'll Never Hear a Dad Say

10.   Well, how 'bout that? I'm lost! Looks like we'll have to stop and ask for directions.

9.   You know Pumpkin, now that you're thirteen, you'll be ready for unchaperoned car dates. Won't that be fun?

8.   I noticed that all your friends have a certain hostile attitude. I like that.

7.   Here's a credit card and the keys to my new car. GO CRAZY!!

6.   What do you mean you wanna play football? Figure skating's not good enough for you, son?

5.   Your Mother and I are going away for the weekend. You might want to consider throwing a party.

4.   Well, I don't know what's wrong with your car. Probably one of those doo-hickey thingies--ya know--that makes it run or something. Just have it towed to a mechanic and pay whatever he asks.

3.   No son of mine is going to live under this roof without an earring. Now quit your bellyaching, and let's go to the mall.

2.   Whaddya wanna go and get a job for? I make plenty of money for you to spend.

1.   What do I want for my birthday? Aahh -- don't worry about that. It's no big deal. (Okay, they might say it. But they don't mean it)

Application for Permission to Date My Daughter

NOTE: This application will be incomplete and rejected unless accompanied by a complete financial statement, job history, lineage, and current medical report from your doctor.

NAME _____

DATE OF BIRTH_____

HEIGHT_____   WEIGHT_____
IQ_____   GPA_____

SOCIAL SECURITY # _____

DRIVERS LICENSE # _____

BOY SCOUT RANK AND
BADGES_____

127

HOME ADDRESS_____

CITY/STATE_____ ZIP_____

Do you have parents?   Yes ____No _____

If No, explain: _____

Number of years they have been married _____

If less than your age, explain _____

Do you own a van? _____

A truck with oversized tires? _____

A waterbed?_____ A pickup with a mattress in the back?_____

Do you have an earring, nose ring, or a belly button ring? _____

A tattoo?_____

(IF YES TO ANY OF THE ABOVE, DISCONTINUE APPLICATION AND
LEAVE PREMISES)

In 50 words or less, what does LATE mean to you?_____

In 50 words or less, what does "DON'T TOUCH MY DAUGHTER" mean to
you? _____

In 50 words or less, what does ABSTINENCE mean to you? _____

Church you attend _____

How often you attend _____

When would be the best time to interview your:

father? _____

mother? _____

pastor? _____

Answer by filling in the blank.   Please answer freely. All answers are
confidential.

A: If I were shot, the last place I would want shot would be: _____

B: If I were beaten, the last bone I would want broken is my: _____

C: A woman's place is in the: _____

D: The one thing I hope this application does not ask me about is:

_____

128

What do you want to do IF you grow up? _____

What is the current going rate of a hotel room? _____

I SWEAR THAT ALL INFORMATION SUPPLIED ABOVE IS TRUE AND CORRECT TO THE BEST OF MY KNOWLEDGE UNDER PENALTY OF DEATH, DISMEMBERMENT, NATIVE AMERICAN ANT TORTURE, ELECTROCUTION, CHINESE WATER TORTURE, AND RED HOT POKERS.

_____

Signature (that means sign your name, goober!)

Thank you for your interest. Please allow four to six years for processing.

You will be contacted in writing if you are approved. Please do not try to call or write (since you probably can't, and it would cause you injury). If your application is rejected, you will be notified by two gentleman wearing white ties carrying violin cases (you might watch your back).

Used Lawn Mower

A preacher retired and moved to the country to enjoy life and practice his hobby of yard work. Needing a lawn mower, he headed into town to buy one. On the way he saw a sign advertising a lawn mower for sale. He stopped at the house and a young lad came out to greet him. The preacher asked about the lawn mower and the kid said it was behind the house. The two went to look at the lawn mower. The engine was sputtering along at idle speed. The preacher increased the speed of the engine and mowed a few strips. Satisfied that the mower would do the job they settled on a price of $25.00.

Later in the day, the young lad was riding his bicycle when he spied the preacher pulling on the engine starter rope. The kid stopped and watched for a couple of minutes. He asked, "What's wrong?"

The reply came, "I can't get this mower started. Do you know how?"

The kid said, "Yep."

"Well, how do you do it? Tell me!" the preacher yelled.

The kid replied, "You have to cuss it."

The preacher rose up indignantly. "Now you listen here. I am a preacher and if I ever did cuss, not saying I have, I've forgotten how to do it after all these years."

With a wise look on his face well beyond his years, the kid said, "Preacher, you keep on pulling that rope and it'll all come back to ya."

Things That Make You Go "ummmmmmmm????"

- If a mute swears, does his mother wash his hands with soap?

- Instead of talking to your plants, if you yelled at them would they still grow? Only to become troubled and insecure?

- Is there another word for synonym?

- Isn't it a bit unnerving that doctors call what they do "practice"?

- When sign makers go on strike, is anything written on their picket signs?

- When you open a bag of cotton balls, is the top one meant to be thrown away?

- Where do forest rangers go to "get away from it all"?

- Why isn't there mouse-flavored cat food?

- Why do they report power outages on TV?

- What do you do when you see an endangered animal that is eating an endangered plant?

- Is it possible to be totally partial?

- What's another word for thesaurus?

- If a parsley farmer is sued, can they garnish his wages?

- Would a fly without wings be called a walk?

- Why do they lock gas station bathrooms? Are they afraid someone will clean them?

- Why do people who know the least know it the loudest?

- If the funeral procession is at night, do folks drive with their headlights off?

- If a stealth bomber crashes in a forest, will it make a sound?

- If a turtle doesn't have a shell, is he homeless or naked?

- When it rains, why don't sheep shrink?

- If the cops arrest a mime, do they tell him he has the right to remain silent?

130

World's Easiest Test

Here is the world's easiest test. You should be able to get 100% on this one.

1. How long did the hundred year war last?

2. Which country makes Panama hats?

3. From what animal do we get catgut?

4. In what month do Russians celebrate the October Revolution?

5. What is Camel's hair brush made from?

6. The Canary Islands in the Pacific are named after what animal?

7. What was King George VI's first name?

8. What color is a Purple Finch?

9. Where are Chinese Gooseberries from?

10. How long did the Thirty Years War last?

That was easy wasn't it? Check the answers below to see how you did. Ready for the answers?

1. 116 years, from 1337 to 1453.

2. Ecuador.

3. From sheep and horses.

4. November. The Russian calendar was 13 days behind ours.

5. Squirrel fur.

6. The Latin name was Insularia Canaria -- Island of the Dogs.

7. Albert. In 1936 he respected the wish of Queen Victoria that no future king should ever be called Albert.

8. Distinctively crimson.

9. New Zealand.

10. 30 years of course. 1618 to 1648.

Before and After Falling in Love

B - You take my breath away
A - I feel like I'm suffocating

131

B - She says she loves the way I take control of the situation
A - She called me a controlling, manipulative egomaniac

B - Lucy and Ricky
A - Fred and Ethel

B - Saturday Night Fever
A - Monday Night Football

B - He makes me feel like a million dollars
A - If I had a dime for every stupid thing he's done...

B - Don't stop
A - Don't start

B - The Sound of Music
A - The Sound of Silence

B - Is that all you're having?
A - Maybe you should just have a salad, honey.

B - Wheel of Fortune
A - Jeopardy

B - It's like I'm in a dream
A - It's like he's in a dorm

B - $60/dozen
A - $1.50/stem

B - Turbo charged
A - Jump start

B - We agree on everything!
A - Doesn't she have a mind of her own?

B - Charming and Noble
A - Chernobyl

B - Idol
A - Idle

B - I love a woman with curves
A - I never said you were fat

B - He's completely lost without me
A - Why won't he ever ask for directions?

B - Time stood still
A - This relationship is going nowhere

B - Croissant and cappuccino
A - Bagel and instant

B - Blind
A - Nearsighted

B - You look so seductive in black
A - Your clothes are so depressing

B - Iambic Pentameter
A - Blank Verse

B - Oysters
A - Fishsticks

B - I can hardly believe we found each other
A - I can't believe I ended up with someone like you

B - Passion
A - Ration

Moose Hunter

Two moose hunters from Texas are flown into a remote lake in Alaska. They have a good hunt, and both manage to get a large moose. When the plane returns to pick them up, the pilot looks at the animals and says, "This little plane won't lift all of us, the equipment, and both of those animals. You'll have to leave one. We'd never make it over the trees on the take off."

"That's bologna," says one of the hunters.

"Yeah," the other agrees, "you're just chicken. We came out here last year and got two moose and that pilot had some guts. He wasn't afraid to take off!"

"Yeah," said the first hunter, "and his plane wasn't any bigger than yours!"

The pilot got angry and said, "If he did it, then I can do it. I can fly as well as anybody!" They loaded up, taxied at full throttle, and the plane almost made it, but didn't have the lift to clear the trees at the end of the lake. It clipped the tops, flipped, then broke up, scattering the baggage, animal carcasses, and passengers all through the brush.

Still alive, but hurt and dazed, the pilot sat up, shook his head to clear it, and said, "Where are we?"

One of the hunters rolled out from being thrown into a bush, looked around, and said, "I'd say about a hundred yards further than last year."

What "Guy" Phrases Really Mean

"I'M GOING FISHING."

really means..."I'm going to go and stand by a stream with a stick in my hand, while the fish swim by in complete safety."

"WOMAN DRIVER."

really means..."Someone who doesn't speed, tailgate, swear, make obscene gestures and has a better driving record than me."

"IT'S A GUY THING."

really means....."There is no rational thought pattern connected with it, and you have no chance at all of making it logical."

"HAVE YOU LOST WEIGHT?"

really means..."I've just spent our last $30 on a cordless drill."

"IT WOULD TAKE TOO LONG TO EXPLAIN."

really means....."I have no idea how it works."

"I GOT A LOT DONE."

really means....."I found 'Waldo' in almost every picture."

"WE'RE GOING TO BE LATE."

really means....."Now I have a legitimate excuse to drive like a maniac."

"TAKE A BREAK, HONEY, YOU'RE WORKING TOO HARD."

really means....."I can't hear the game over the vacuum cleaner."

"HONEY, WE DON'T NEED MATERIAL THINGS TO PROVE OUR LOVE."

really means....."I forgot our anniversary again."

"YOU KNOW HOW BAD MY MEMORY IS."

really means....."I remember the theme song to 'F Troop' and the Vehicle Identification Numbers on every car I've ever owned, but I forgot your birthday."

"HEY I'VE GOT MY REASONS FOR WHAT I'M DOING."

really means....."And I sure hope I think of some pretty soon."

"I CAN'T FIND IT."

really means....."It didn't fall into my outstretched hands, so I'm completely clueless."

"WHAT DID I DO THIS TIME?"

really means...."What did you catch me at?"

"I DON'T NEED TO READ THE INSTRUCTIONS."

really means....."I am perfectly capable of screwing it up without printed help."

"I'M NOT LOST. I KNOW EXACTLY WHERE WE ARE."

really means....."No one will ever see us alive again."

Speeding Stories

PULLED OVER

"Hey you! Pull over!" shouted the traffic cop.

The lady complied, and the judge next day fined her twenty-five dollars. She went home in great anxiety lest her husband, who always examined her checkbook, should learn of the incident. Then inspiration struck and she marked the check stub, "One pullover, $25."

WHY ME?

My friend Walt was driving a rig in a long line of tractor-trailers when a police officer pulled him over for speeding. Astounded that he alone was caught, he asked, "Out of all these trucks that were going just as fast as I was, why did you pull me over?"

"Have you ever gone fishing?" the officer asked.

"Yes," Walt replied.

"Well, have you ever caught all the fish in the pond?"

SPEEDING

The police have stopped my husband so many times for speeding, they decided to just give him a season ticket.

TWO SPEED CORVETTE

Nick lives in a subdivision that branches off the main highway. He drives a Corvette, and thinks the only two speeds are "STOP" and "FULL SPEED."

One day, when he was late for work, he comes tearing out the road from his house, tops the little hill before getting to the main road, and sees a police car blocking the road. He slams on the brakes and comes to a screeching halt about 6 inches from the police car. The policeman, who had often

135

seen him driving fast, walked up and said, "Mister, I've been waiting for you all morning..."

Nick replied, "Well, I got here as fast as I could!"

Newspaper Ads

These are real ads from a newspaper.

1 MAN, 7 WOMAN HOT TUB -- $850 OR BEST OFFER

AMANA WASHER $100. OWNED BY CLEAN BACHELOR WHO SELDOM WASHED.

SNOW BLOWER FOR SALE...ONLY USED ON SNOWY DAYS.

FREE PUPPIES...PART GERMAN SHEPHERD, PART DOG.

2 WIRE MESH BUTCHERING GLOVES, 1 5-finger, 1 3-finger, PAIR: $15

TICKLE ME ELMO, STILL IN BOX, COMES WITH IT'S OWN 1988 MUSTANG, AUTO TRANS., EXCELLENT CONDITION - $6800

DO SOMETHING SPECIAL FOR YOUR VALENTINE - HAVE YOUR SEPTIC TANK PUMPED

FREE PUPPIES: 1/2 COCKER SPANIEL - 1/2 SNEAKY NEIGHBOR DOG

FREE YORKSHIRE TERRIER. 8 YEARS OLD, UNPLEASANT LITTLE DOG

GERMAN SHEPHERD. 85 lbs. NEUTERED. SPEAKS GERMAN. FREE.

FREE - 1 CAN OF PORK & BEANS WITH PURCHASE OF 3 BR 2 BATH HOME.

NORDIC TRAC $300 - HARDLY USED - CALL CHUBBIE AT:

BILL'S SEPTIC CLEANING - "WE HAUL AMERICAN MADE PRODUCTS"

FOUND: DIRTY WHITE DOG...LOOKS LIKE A RAT...BEEN OUT AWHILE...BETTER BE A REWARD

HUMMELS - LARGEST SELECTION - "IF IT'S IN STOCK, WE HAVE IT"

CUTE KITTEN FOR SALE, 2 CENTS OR BEST OFFER

WHIRLPOOL BUILT IN OVEN -- FROST FREE!

'93 PONTIAC LEMONS - LOW MILES

KITTENS 8 WEEKS OLD - SEEKING GOOD CHRISTIAN HOME.

TIRED OF WORKING FOR ONLY $9.75 PER HOUR? WE OFFER PROFIT SHARING AND FLEXIBLE HOURS. STARTING PAY: $7 - $9 PER HOUR.

Shopkeeper's Competition

The shopkeeper was dismayed when a brand new business much like his own opened up next door and erected a huge sign which read BEST DEALS.

He was horrified when another competitor opened up on his right, and announced its arrival with an even larger sign, reading LOWEST PRICES.

The shopkeeper was panicked, until he got an idea. He put the biggest sign of all over his own shop. It read...

MAIN ENTRANCE.

Wayward Cessna

You've all heard of the Air Force's ultra-high security, super-secret base in Nevada, known simply as "Area 51?"

Well, late one afternoon, the Air Force folks out at Area 51 were very surprised to see a Cessna landing at their "secret" base. They immediately impounded the aircraft and hauled the pilot into an interrogation room.

The pilot's story was that he took off from Vegas, got lost, and spotted the Base just as he was about to run out of fuel. The Air Force started a full FBI background check on the pilot and held him overnight during the investigation.

By the next day, they were finally convinced that the pilot really was lost and wasn't a spy. They gassed up his airplane, gave him a terrifying "you-did-not-see-a-base" briefing, complete with threats of spending the rest of his life in prison, told him Vegas was that-a-way on such-and-such a heading, and sent him on his way.

The next day, to the total disbelief of the Air Force, the same Cessna showed up again. Once again, the MP's surrounded the plane...only this time there were two people in the plane.

The same pilot jumped out and said, "Do anything you want to me, but my wife is in the plane and you have to tell her where I was last night!"

Goober Travelers

The following are actual stories provided by travel agents:

* I had someone ask for an aisle seat so that their hair wouldn't get messed up by being near the window.

* A client called in inquiring about a package to Hawaii. After going over all the cost info, she asked, "Would it be cheaper to fly to California and then take the train to Hawaii?"

* I got a call from a woman who wanted to go to Cape Town. I started to explain the length of the flight and the passport information when she interrupted me with "I'm not trying to make you look stupid, but Cape Town is in Massachusetts." Without trying to make her look like the stupid one, I calmly explained, "Cape Cod is in Massachusetts, Cape Town is in Africa." Her response ... click.

* A man called, furious about a Florida package we did. I asked what was wrong with the vacation in Orlando. He said he was expecting an ocean-view room. I tried to explain that is not possible, since Orlando is in the middle of the state. He replied, "Don't lie to me. I looked on the map and Florida is a very thin state."

* I got a call from a man who asked, "Is it possible to see England from Canada?" I said, "No." He said, "But they look so close on the map."

* Another man called and asked if he could rent a car in Dallas. When I pulled up the reservation, I noticed he had a 1-hour layover in Dallas.

When I asked him why he wanted to rent a car, he said, "I heard Dallas was a big airport, and I need a car to drive between the gates to save time."

* A nice lady just called. She needed to know how it was possible that her flight from Detroit left at 8:20am and got into Chicago at 8:33am. I tried to explain that Michigan was an hour ahead of Illinois, but she could not understand the concept of time zones. Finally I told her the plane went very fast, and she bought that!

* A woman called and asked, "Do airlines put your physical description on your bag so they know whose luggage belongs to who?" I said, "No, why do you ask?" She replied, "Well, when I checked in with the airline, they put a tag on my luggage that said FAT, and I'm overweight. Is there any connection?"

After putting her on hold for a minute while "I looked into it," (I was actually laughing) I came back and explained that the city code for Fresno is FAT, and that the airline was just putting a destination tag on her luggage.

* I just got off the phone with a man who asked, "How do I know which plane to get on?" I asked him what exactly he meant, to which he replied, "I was told my flight number is 823, but none of these darn planes have numbers on them."

* A woman called and said, "I need to fly to Pepsi-cola on one of those computer planes." I asked if she meant to fly

138

to Pensacola on a commuter plane. She said, "Yeah, whatever."

* A business man called and had a question about the documents he needed in order to fly to China. After a lengthy discussion about passports, I reminded him he needed a visa. "Oh no I don't, I've been to China many times and never had to have one of those." I double-checked and sure enough, his stay required a visa. When I told him this he said, "Look, I've been to China four times and every time they have accepted my American Express."

* A woman called to make reservations; "I want to go from Chicago to Hippopotamus, New York." The agent was at a loss for words. Finally, the agent asked, "Are you sure that's the name of the town?" "Yes, what flights do you have?" replied the customer. After some searching, the agent came back with, "I'm sorry, ma'am. I've looked up every airport code in the country and can't find a Hippopotamus anywhere." The customer retorted, "Oh, don't be silly. Everyone knows where it is. Check your map!" The agent scoured a map of the state of New York and finally offered, "You don't mean Buffalo, do you?" "That's it! I knew it was a big animal!"

Heat Wave Jokes

Nothing personal against Texans - change it to any place that is hot.

"It's So Hot In Texas That......"

*The birds have to use potholders to pull worms out of the ground.

*The potatoes cook underground. All you have to do to have lunch is pull one out then add butter, salt and pepper.

*Farmers are feeding their chickens crushed ice to keep them from laying hard-boiled eggs.

*The cows are giving evaporated milk.

*The trees are whistling for the dogs.

*A sad Texan once prayed, "I wish it would rain - not so much for me, cuz I've seen it - but for my 7-year-old."

*A visitor to Texas once asked, "Does it ever rain out here?" A rancher quickly answered, "Yes, it does. Do you remember that part in the Bible where it rained for 40 days and 40 nights?" The visitor replied, "Yes, I'm familiar with Noah's flood." "Well," the rancher puffed up, "we got about two and a half inches of that."

"You Know You're In Texas When..."

*You no longer associate bridges (or rivers) with water.

139

*You can say 110 degrees without fainting.

*You eat hot chilies to cool your mouth off.

*You can make instant sun tea.

*You learn that a seat belt makes a pretty good branding iron.

*The temperature drops below 95, you feel a bit chilly.

*You discover that in July, it takes only 2 fingers to drive your car.

*You discover that you can get a sunburn through your car window.

*You notice the best parking place is determined by shade instead of distance.

*Hot water now comes out of both taps.

*It's noon in July, kids are on summer vacation, and not one person is out on the streets.

*You actually burn your hand opening the car door.

*You break into a sweat the instant you step outside at 7:30 a.m.

*No one would dream of putting vinyl upholstery in a car or not having air conditioning.

*Your biggest bicycle wreck fear is, "What if I get knocked out and end up lying on the pavement and cook to death?"

*You realize that asphalt has a liquid state.

Rainy Weather Jokes

Nothing personal against Seattleites - change it to any other place getting a lot of rain.

- A newcomer to Seattle arrives on a rainy day. She gets up the next day and it's raining. It also rains the day after that, and the day after that. She goes out to lunch and sees a young kid and out of despair asks, "Hey kid, does it ever stop raining around here?" The kid says, "How should I know? I'm only 6."

- "I can't believe it," said the tourist. "I've been here an entire week and it's done nothing but rain. When do you have summer here?" "Well, that's hard to say, " replied the local. "Last year, it was on a Wednesday."

- Q. What do you call two straight days of rain in Seattle?
  A. A weekend.

- What did the Seattle native say to the Pillsbury Doughboy?
  "Nice tan."

- Did you know that Cinderella was a Seattle native?
  Who else would need a fairy (ferry) to get to the ball?

- Meteorological experts were predicting a gargantuan flood that would destroy the world. The Pope went on worldwide TV and said, "This is punishment from God. Prepare to meet your Maker." The President went on national TV and announced, "Our scientists have done all they can. The end is near." The Seattle evening news came on and said, "Today's five day forecast - same as usual."

- What does daylight savings time mean in Seattle?
  An extra hour of rain.

- It rains only twice a year in Seattle.
  August to April and May to July.

Human Resource Help

What is a human resource? Does your organization struggle with the problem of properly fitting people to jobs? Here is a handy hint for ensuring success in job placement:

Take the prospective employees you are trying to place and put them in a room with only a table and two chairs. Leave them alone for two hours, without any instruction. At the end of that time, go back and see what they are doing.

If they have taken the table apart in that time, put them in Engineering.

If they are counting the butts in the ashtray, assign them to Finance.

If they are screaming and waving their arms, send them to Manufacturing.

If they are talking to the chairs, Personnel is a good spot for them.

If they are sleeping, they are Management material.

If they are writing up the experience, send them to Technical Publications.

If they don't even look up when you enter the room, assign them to Security.

If they try to tell you it's not as bad as it looks, send them to Marketing.

And if they've left early, put them in Sales.

Prized Pet Pig

Farmer Jones got out of his car and while heading for his friend's door, noticed a pig with a wooden leg. His curiosity roused, he ask, "Fred, how'd that pig get him a wooden leg?"

"Well Michael, that's a mighty special pig! A while back a wild boar attacked me while I was walking in the woods. That pig there came a runnin', went after that boar and chased him away. Saved my life!"

"And the boar tore up his leg?"

"No he was fine after that. But a bit later we had that fire. Started in the shed up against the barn. Well, that ole pig started squealin' like he was stuck, woke us up, and 'fore we got out here, the darn thing had herded the other animals out of the barn and saved 'em all!"

"So that's when he hurt his leg, huh, Fred?"

"No, Michael. He was a might winded, though. When my tractor hit a rock and rolled down the hill into the pond I was knocked clean out. When I came to, that pig had dove into the pond and dragged me out 'fore I drownded. Sure did save my life."

"And that was when he hurt his leg?"

"Oh no, he was fine. Cleaned him up, too."

"OK, Fred. So just tell me. How did he get the wooden leg?"

"Well", the farmer tells him, "a pig like that, you don't want to eat all at once!"

Are You Tired of Reading?

WASHINGTON, DC--Decrying needlessly confusing directions for the use and assembly of countless products, citizens across the nation are organizing advocacy groups to demand that American manufacturers simplify the instructions they place on packaging.

"I'm a busy father of three," said Richard Graham of Chester, VA. "I don't have time to wade through all those words and confusing pictures on the box of flavored instant-oatmeal packets. Why can't I just get the bowl of hot oatmeal without going through so much trouble?"

On behalf of dissatisfied consumers like Graham, the Washington-based activist group Citizens for Easier Instructions has delivered an ultimatum to corporations: Replace current directions with easier versions or face a consumer boycott.

"We demand that product manufacturers provide their customers with intuitive, easy-to-follow directions featuring larger pictures, color coding, shorter words, and no words at all where a letter, number or pictograph would suffice," CEI director Melanie Pruitt said Tuesday at a press conference kicking off the group's "Crusade For Clarity '99" campaign.

"For too long, the people of America have stared blankly at monochromatic, densely printed lines of instructions on cans, bottles and boxes, straining to digest the elaborately worded directives. We say, 'no more.'"

Pruitt, who nets a six-figure salary as one of the country's top instruction-clarity advocates, then unveiled a large placard showing the multi-step instructions on a can of Chef Boyardee beef ravioli.

"The first instruction, 'Empty contents into saucepan,' is only the first problem with this mind-bogglingly Byzantine label," Pruitt said. "No clue is offered on how to retrieve these 'contents' from the hard, silvery shell surrounding them. In fact, our research staff has determined that a tool not included with the can is necessary."

Moving further along the label, Pruitt noted additional directions that would pose comprehension problems for the average consumer: "'Stir occasionally until hot,' the label instructs. How often is 'occasionally'? If I only prepare ravioli 'occasionally,' should I not stir at all?"

Perhaps the label's most confusing factor, Pruitt said, was the existence of two separate series of instructions, depending on the heating device used.

"The already-baffling 'Stir occasionally until hot' is not even properly identified as the final instruction in the stove-top-specific set of instructions before the text flows right into the second set, making the cook think that the next step in the preparation process is 'Microwave,'" Pruitt said. "The second set of instructions is even more paradoxical, demanding such tasks as, 'Stir once during heating,' despite the fact that the food product is heated in a microwave which ceases to function if it is opened to get at the food."

To avoid a consumer boycott, Pruitt recommended that the maker of Chef Boyardee print the words, "Requires can opener, saucepan, stove and electrical power" on the front of every label in large letters, and present the instructions in the form of pictographs showing a gender-neutral stick figure traveling sequentially through all the steps of preparation, from opening the can to emptying the product into the saucepan, all through the cooking process, transferring the contents from the saucepan to a serving dish, and finally consuming the food using appropriate utensils.

"We believe the entire process can be rendered in as few as 22 pictographs, which could be large enough to be easily read if printed on the inside of the label," Pruitt said. "All that would be needed is an exterior instruction directing the preparer to remove the label and read the full, interior instruction set."

"Corporations that fail to respond to the changing needs of Americans will lose customers," she added. "We as a people no longer have the time or patience to read lines of text and struggle to decipher their meaning."

Manufacturer Procter & Gamble has already announced it will soon introduce new "EZ 2 Follow" instructions that will clearly spell out "even the simplest and most obvious of operations."

The redesigned Old Spice aftershave lotion bottle, company representative Albert Conrad said, will feature explicit instructions regarding where and how to apply the lotion, as well as warnings not to drink Old Spice or use it as a marinade in cooking.

Sheets included in other Procter & Gamble products will warn against eating Crisco straight from the can, squirting Vicks Nyquil into one's eyes, or re-using Band-Aids products.

Many other corporations have already made moves toward similar changes based on the overwhelming number of questions and complaints they receive at their 800 numbers every day.

"I used to answer 30 to 40 calls a day from people asking what 'Apply liberally' meant," said Carla Enway, an operator for Coppertone. "My job has been a lot easier since we changed the bottle to read, "Spread a whole bunch all over everything but your eyes and mouth."

Earliest Tech Support

The tech support problem dates back to long before the industrial revolution, when primitive tribesmen beat out a rhythm on drums to communicate:

This fire help. Me Groog.

Me Lorto. Help. Fire not work.

You have flint and stone?

Ugh.

You hit them together?

Ugh.

What happen?

Fire not work (sigh).

Make spark?

No spark, no fire, me confused. Fire work yesterday.

sigh You change rock?

I change nothing.

You sure?

Me make one change. Stone hot so me soak in stream so stone not burn Lorto hand. Small change, shouldn't keep Lorto from make fire.

Grabs club and goes to Lorto's cave

Philosophy of Love...

If you love something, set it free.

If it comes back, it will always be yours.

If it doesn't come back, it was never yours to begin with.

But... If it just sits in your living room, watches your TV, messes up your stuff, eats your food, uses your telephone, takes your money, and doesn't appear to realize that you actually set it free in the first place, you either married it or gave birth to it!

Sales Call

(Thanks to R. Byron of absoluterobeo.com for permission to reprint this.)

One thing that has always bugged me, and I'm sure it does most of you, is to sit down at the dinner table only to be interrupted by a phone call from a telemarketer. I decided, on one such occasion, to try to be as irritating as they were to me. The call was from AT&T and it went something like this:

Me: Hello

AT&T: Hello, this is AT&T...

Me: Is this AT&T?

AT&T: Yes, this is AT&T...

Me: This is AT&T?

AT&T: Yes. This is AT&T...

Me: Is this AT&T?

AT&T: YES! This is AT&T; may I speak to Mr. Byron please?

Me: May I ask who is calling?

AT&T: This is AT&T.

Me: OK, hold on.

At this point I put the phone down for a solid 5 minutes thinking that, surely, this person would have hung up the phone. Much to my surprise, when I picked up the receiver, they were still waiting.

Me: Hello?

AT&T: Is this Mr. Byron?

Me: May I ask who is calling please?

AT&T: Yes this is AT&T...

Me: Is this AT&T?

AT&T: Yes this is AT&T...

Me: This is AT&T?

AT&T: Yes, is this Mr. Byron?

Me: Yes, is this AT&T?

AT&T: Yes sir.

Me: The phone company?

AT&T: Yes sir.

Me: I thought you said this is AT&T.

AT&T: Yes sir, we are a phone company.

Me: I already have a phone.

AT&T: We aren't selling phones today Mr. Byron.

Me: Well whatever it is, I'm really not interested but thanks for calling.

When you are not interested in something, I don't think you can express yourself any plainer than by saying "I'm really not interested", but this lady was persistent.

AT&T: Mr. Byron we would like to offer you 10 cents a minute, 24 hours a day, 7 days a week, 365 days a year.

Now, I am sure she meant she was offering a "rate" of 10 cents a minute but she at no time used the word rate. I could clearly see that it was time to whip out the trusty old calculator and do a little ciphering.

Me: Now, that's 10 cents a minute 24 hours a day?

AT&T: (getting a little excited at this point by my interest) Yes sir, that's right! 24 hours a day!

Me: 7 days a week?

AT&T: That's right.

Me: 365 days a year?

AT&T: Yes sir.

Me: I am definitely interested in that! Wow!!! That's amazing!

AT&T: We think so!

Me: That's quite a sum of money!

AT&T: Yes sir, it's amazing how it adds up.

Me: OK, so will you send me checks weekly, monthly or just one big one at the end of the year for the full $52,560, and if you send an annual check, can I get a cash advance?

AT&T: Excuse me?

Me: You know, the 10 cents a minute.

AT&T: What are you talking about?

Me: You said you'd give me 10 cents a minute, 24 hours a day, 7 days a week, 365 days a year. That comes to $144 per day, $1008 per week and $52,560 per year. I'm just interested in knowing how you will be making payment.

AT&T: Oh no sir I didn't mean we'd be paying you. You pay us 10 cents a minute.

Me: Wait a minute here!!! Didn't you say you'd give me 10 cents a minute? Are you sure this is AT&T?

AT&T: Well, yes this is AT&T sir but......

Me: But nothing, how do you figure that by saying that you'll give me 10 cents a minute that I'll give you 10 cents a minute? Is this some kind of subliminal telemarketing scheme? I've read about things like this in the Enquirer you know. Don't use your alien brainwashing techniques on me.

AT&T: No sir, we are offering 10 cents a minute for.....

Me: THERE YOU GO AGAIN! Can I speak to a supervisor please!

AT&T: Sir, I don't think that is necessary.

Me: Sure! You say that now! What happens later?

AT&T: What?

Me: I insist on speaking to a supervisor!

AT&T: Yes Mr. Byron. Please hold on.

So now AT&T has me on hold and my supper is getting cold. I begin to eat while I'm waiting for a supervisor. After

147

a wait of a few minutes and while I have a mouth full of food:

Supervisor: Mr. Byron?

Me: Yeth?

Supervisor: I understand you are not quite understanding our 10 cents a minute program.

Me: Id thish Ath Teeth & Teeth?

Supervisor: Yes sir, it sure is.

I had to swallow before I choked on my food. It was all I could do to suppress my laughter and I had to be careful not to produce a snort.

Me: No, actually I was just waiting for someone to get back to me so that I could sign up for the plan.

Supervisor: OK, no problem, I'll transfer you back to the person who was helping you.

Me: Thank you.

I was on hold once again and was getting really hungry. I needed to end this conversation. Suddenly, there was an aggravated but polite voice at the other end of the phone.

AT&T: Hello Mr. Byron, I understand that you are interested in signing up for our plan?

Me: Do you have that friends and family thing because you can never have enough friends and I'm an only child and I'd really like to have a little brother...

AT&T: (click)

Training Courses Now Available for Men

- Introduction to Common Household Objects I: The Mop

- Introduction to Common Household Objects II: The Sponge

- Dressing Up: Beyond the Funeral and the Wedding

- Refrigerator Forensics: Identifying and Removing the Dead

- Design Pattern or Splatter Stain on the Linoleum?: You CAN Tell the Difference!

- Accepting Loss I: If It's Empty, You Can Throw It Away

- Accepting Loss II: If the Milk Expired Three Weeks Ago, Keeping It In the Refrigerator Won't Bring It Back

- Going to the Supermarket: It's Not Just for Women Anymore!

- Recycling Skills I: Boxes that the Electronics Came In

- Recycling Skills II: Styrofoam that Came in the Boxes that the Electronics Came In

- Bathroom Etiquette I: How to Remove Beard Clippings from the Sink

- Bathroom Etiquette II: Let's Wash Those Towels!

- Bathroom Etiquette III: Five Easy Ways to Tell When You're About to Run Out of Toilet Paper!

- Giving Back to the Community: How to Donate 15-Year-Old Levis to the Goodwill

- Retro? Or Just Hideous?: Re-examining Your 1970's Polyester Shirts

- Knowing the Limitations of Your Kitchenware: No, The Dishes Won't Wash Themselves

- Romance: More Than a Cable Channel!

- Strange But True!: She Really May NOT Care What "Fourth Down and Ten" Means

- Going Out to Dinner: Beyond the Pizza Hut

- Expand Your Entertainment Options: Renting Movies That Don't Fall Under the "Action/Adventure" Category

- Yours, Mine, and Ours: Sharing the Remote

- "I Could Have Played a Better Game Than That!": Why Women Laugh

- Adventures in Housekeeping I: Let's Clean the Closet

- Adventures in Housekeeping II: Let's Clean Under the Bed

- "I Don't Know": Be the First Man to Say It!

- The Gas Gauge in Your Car: Sometimes Empty MEANS Empty

- Directions: It's Okay to Ask for Them

- Listening: It's Not Just Something You Do During Halftime

- Accepting Your Limitations: Just Because You Have Power Tools Doesn't Mean You Can Fix It

Useful Work Phrases (to Say in Your Head)

- Thank you. We're all refreshed and challenged by your unique point of view.

- I like you. You remind me of when I was young and clued out.

- Someday, we'll look back on this, laugh nervously and change the subject.

- I will always cherish the initial misconceptions I had about you.

- Ahhh ... I see the mess-up fairy has visited us again...

- I'm already visualizing the duct tape over your mouth.

- How about never? Is never good for you?

- The fact that no one understands you doesn't mean you're an artist.

- I don't know what your problem is, but I'll bet it's hard to pronounce.

- Any connection between your reality and mine is purely coincidental.

- What am I? Flypaper for goobers!

- I see you've set aside this special time to humiliate yourself in public.

- No, my powers can only be used for good.

- My toys! My toys! I can't do this job without my toys!

- I'll try being nicer if you'll try being smarter.

- I'm out of my mind, but feel free to leave a message...

- I don't work here. I'm a consultant.

- At least I have a positive attitude about my destructive habits.

- Who me? I just wander from room to room.

- It might look like I'm doing nothing, but at the cellular level I'm really quite busy.

Where Are We?

Two tourists were driving through Louisiana. As they were approaching Natchitoches, they started arguing about the pronunciation of the town.

They argued back and forth until they stopped for lunch. As they stood at the counter, one tourist asked a goober employee, "Before we order, could you please settle an argument for us? Would you please pronounce where we are... very slowly?"

The Goober leaned over the counter and said, "Burrrrrrrr-gerrrrrrr-Kiiiiing."

Things I've Learned From My Children

Things I've learned from my children (honest and no kidding):

- There is no such thing as child-proofing your house.

- If you spray hair spray on dust bunnies and run over them with roller blades, they can ignite.

- A 4 year-old's voice is louder than 200 adults in a crowded restaurant.

- If you hook a dog leash over a ceiling fan the motor is not strong enough to rotate a 42 pound boy wearing pound puppy underwear and a superman cape.

- It is strong enough however to spread paint on all four walls of a 20 by 20 foot room.

- Baseballs make marks on ceilings.

- You should not throw baseballs up when the ceiling fan is on.

- When using the ceiling fan as a bat you have to throw the ball up a few times before you get a hit.

- A ceiling fan can hit a baseball a long way.

- The glass in windows (even double paned) doesn't stop a baseball hit by a ceiling fan.

- When you hear the toilet flush and then, "Uh-oh," it's already too late.

- Brake fluid mixed with Clorox makes smoke, and lots of it.

- A six year old can start a fire with a flint rock even though a 36-year-old man says they can only do it in the movies.

- A magnifying glass can start a fire even on an overcast day.

- If you use a waterbed as home plate while wearing baseball shoes it does not leak, it explodes.

- A king size waterbed holds enough water to fill a 2000 sq foot house 4 inches deep.

- Lego will pass through the digestive tract of a four year old.

- Duplo will not.

- Play Dough and Microwave should never be used in the same sentence.

- Super glue is forever.

- McGyver can teach us many things we don't want to know.

- Ditto Tarzan.

- No matter how much Jell-O you put in a swimming pool you still can't walk on water.

- Pool filters do not like Jell-O.

- VCR's do not eject PB&J sandwiches even though TV commercials show they do.

- Garbage bags do not make good parachutes.

- Marbles in gas tanks make lots of noise when driving.

- You probably do not want to know what that odor is.

- Always look in the oven before you turn it on.

- Plastic toys do not like ovens.

- The fire department in San Diego has at least a 5-minute response time.

- The spin cycle on the washing machine does not make earthworms dizzy.

- It will however make cats dizzy.

- Cats throw up twice their body weight when dizzy.

- A good sense of humor will get you through most problems in life (unfortunately, mostly in retrospect).

Priest's Uniform

A little boy, not accustomed to seeing a priest in his "work uniform" went up to the priest and asked, "Why do you dress so funny?" The priest replied, "This is the uniform that I wear when I work."

The child, still staring at him, asked, "Do you have a boo boo?" The priest was somewhat puzzled, but quickly figured out that the child was looking at his white and black Roman collar. The priest pulled out the white plastic insert and showed it to the child telling him that it was also part of his uniform.

On the back side of the collar there was some writing: "Wash with warm soapy water." The priest showed this to the little boy and then asked him "Do you know what these words say?"

The little boy, obviously much too young to read, stated, "I sure do."

The priest a little taken aback replied, "OK then, tell me what they say."

The little boy then replies, "Kills fleas and ticks for up to six months."

Fortunate Aged People

Dear Son, I am writing to tell you that as I age I have discovered that old folks are worth a fortune with silver in their hair, gold in their teeth, stones in their kidneys, lead in their feet and gas in their stomachs.

I have become more social with the passing of the years; some might even call me a frivolous old gal. I'm seeing five gentlemen everyday.

As soon as I wake, Will Power helps me get out of bed. Then I go see John. Then Charley Horse comes along, and when he is here he takes a lot of my time and attention. When he leaves, Arthur Ritis shows up and stays the rest of the day. (He doesn't like to stay in one place very long, so he takes me from joint to joint.) After such a busy day, I'm really tired and glad to go to bed - with Ben Gay. What a life!

P.S. The preacher came to call the other day. He said that at my age I should be thinking about the hereafter. I told him I do - all the time. No matter where I am - in the parlor, upstairs in the kitchen or down in the basement - I ask myself, "Now, what am I here after?"

Strange Exam Answers

- Ancient Egypt was inhabited by mummies and they all wrote in hydraulics. They lived in the Sarah Dessert and traveled by Camelot. The climate of the Sarah is such that the inhabitants have to live elsewhere.

- The Bible is full of interesting caricatures. In the first book of the Bible, Guinessis, Adam and Eve were created from an apple tree. One of their children, Cain, asked, "Am I my brother's son?"

- Moses led the Hebrew slaves to the Red Sea, where they made unleavened bread which is bread made without any ingredients. Moses went up on Mount Cyanide to get the Ten Commandments. He died before he ever reached Canada.

- Solomom had three hundred wives and seven hundred porcupines.

- The Greeks were a highly sculptured people, and without them we wouldn't have history. The Greeks also had myths. A myth is a female moth.

- Actually, Homer was not written by Homer but by another man of that name.

- Socrates was a famous Greek teacher who went around giving people advice. They killed him. Socrates died from an overdose of wedlock. After his death, his career suffered a dramatic decline.

- In the Olympic games, Greeks ran races, jumped, hurled the biscuits, and threw the java.

- Eventually, the Romans conquered the Greeks. History calls people Romans because they never stayed in one place for very long.

- Julius Caesar extinguished himself on the battlefields of Gaul. The Ides of March murdered him because they thought he was going to be made king. Dying, he gasped out: "Tee hee, Brutus."

- Nero was a cruel tyranny who would torture his subjects by playing the fiddle to them.

- Joan of Arc was burnt to a steak and was canonized by Bernard Shaw. Finally Magna Carta provided that no man should be hanged twice for the same offense.

- In midevil times most people were alliterate. The greatest writer of the futile ages was Chaucer, who wrote many poems and verses and also wrote literature.

- Another story was William Tell, who shot an arrow through an apple while standing on his son's head.

- Queen Elizabeth was the "Virgin Queen." As a queen she was a success. When she exposed herself before her troops they all shouted "hurrah."

154

- It was an age of great inventions and discoveries. Gutenberg invented removable type and the Bible. Another important invention was the circulation of blood. Sir Walter Raleigh is a historical figure because he invented cigarettes and started smoking. And Sir Francis Drake circumcised the world with a 100-foot clipper.

- The greatest writer of the Renaissance was William Shakespeare. He was born in the year 1564, supposedly on his birthday. He never made much money and is famous only because of his plays. He wrote tragedies, comedies, and hysterectomies, all in Islamic pentameter. Romeo and Juliet are an example of a heroic couplet. Romeo's last wish was to be laid by Juliet.

- Writing at the same time as Shakespeare was Miguel Cervantes. He wrote Donkey Hote. The next great author was John Milton. Milton wrote Paradise Lost. Then his wife died and he wrote Paradise Regained.

- During the Renaissance America began. Christopher Columbus was a great navigator who discovered America while cursing about the Atlantic. His ships were called the Nina, the Pinta, and the Santa Fe.

- Later, the Pilgrims crossed the ocean, and this was called Pilgrim's Progress. The winter of 1620 was a hard one for the settlers. Many people died and many babies were born. Captain John Smith was responsible for all this.

- One of the causes of the Revolutionary War was the English put tacks in their tea. Also, the colonists would send their parcels through the post without stamps. Finally the colonists won the War and no longer had to pay for taxis. Delegates from the original 13 states formed the Contented Congress. Thomas Jefferson, a Virgin, and Benjamin Franklin were two singers of the Declaration of Independence. Franklin discovered electricity by rubbing two cats backwards and declared, "A horse divided against itself cannot stand." Franklin died in 1790 and is still dead.

- Soon the Constitution of the United States was adopted to secure domestic hostility. Under the constitution the people enjoyed the right to keep bare arms.

- Abraham Lincoln became America's greatest Precedent. Lincoln's mother died in infancy, and he was born in a log cabin which he built with his own hands. Abraham Lincoln freed the slaves by signing the Emasculation Proclamation. On the night of April 14, 1865, Lincoln went to the theater and got shot in his seat by one of the actors in a moving picture show. The believed assinator was John Wilkes Booth, a supposedly insane actor. This ruined Booth's career.

- Meanwhile in Europe, the enlightenment was a reasonable time. Voltaire invented electricity and also wrote a book called Candy.

- Gravity was invented by Issac Walton. It is chiefly noticeable in the autumn when the apples are falling off the trees.

- Johann Bach wrote a great many musical compositions and had a large number of children. In between he practiced on an old spinster which he kept up in his attic. Bach died from 1750 to the present. Bach was the most famous composer in the world and so was Handel. Handel was half German half Italian and half English. He was very large.

- Beethoven wrote music even though he was deaf. He was so deaf he wrote loud music. He took long walks in the forest even when everyone was calling for him. Beethoven expired in 1827 and later died for this.

- The French Revolution was accomplished before it happened and catapulted into Napoleon. Napoleon wanted an heir to inherit his power, but since Josephine was a baroness, she couldn't have any children.

- The sun never set on the British Empire because the British Empire is in the East and the sun sets in the West.

- Queen Victoria was the longest queen. She sat on a thorn for 63 years. She was a moral woman who practiced virtue. Her death was the final event which ended her reign.

- Louis Pasteur discovered a cure for rabbis. Charles Darwin was a naturalist who wrote the Organ of the Species. Madman Curie discovered radio. And Karl Marx became one of the Marx brothers.

- The First World War, caused by the assignation of the Arch-Duck by an anahist, ushered in a new error in the anals of human history.

WHAT TO DO WITH ALL THOSE "FREE" SOAPS WHEN TRAVELLING

(I have saved one of my absolute favorite CleanLaughs 'til last.)

Dear Maid, Please do not leave any more of those little bars of soap in my bathroom since I have brought my own bath-sized Dial. Please remove the six unopened little bars from the shelf under the medicine chest and another three in the shower soap dish. They are in my way.

Thank you, S. Berman

Dear Room 635, I am not your regular maid. She will be back tomorrow, Thursday, from her day off. I took the 3 hotel soaps out of the shower soap dish as you requested. The 6 bars on your shelf I took out of your way and put on top of your Kleenex dispenser in case you should change your mind. This leaves only the 3 bars I left today, as my instructions from management are to leave 3 soaps daily. I hope this is satisfactory.

Kathy, Relief Maid

Dear Maid, I hope you are my regular maid. Apparently Kathy did not tell you about my note to her concerning the little bars of soap. When I got back to my room this evening I found you had added 3 little Camays to the shelf under my medicine cabinet. I am going to be here in the hotel for two weeks and have brought my own bath-sized Dial so I won't need those 6 little Camays which are on the shelf. They are in my way when shaving, brushing teeth, etc. Please remove them.

S. Berman

Dear Mr. Berman, My day off was last Wed. so the relief maid left 3 hotel soaps, which the management instructs us to do. I took the 6 soaps that were in your way on the shelf and put them in the soap dish where your Dial was. I put the Dial in the medicine cabinet for your convenience. I didn't remove the 3 complimentary soaps which are always placed inside the medicine cabinet for all new check-ins and which you did not object to when you checked in last Monday. Please let me know if I can be of further assistance.

Your regular maid, Dotty

Dear Mr. Berman, The assistant manager, Mr. Kensedder, informed me this A.M. that you called him last evening and said you were unhappy with your maid service. I have assigned a new girl to your room. I hope you will accept my apologies for any past inconvenience. If you have any future complaints please contact me so I can give it my personal attention. Call extension 1108 between 8AM and 5PM. Thank you.

Elaine Carmen, Housekeeper

Dear Miss Carmen, It is impossible to contact you by phone since I leave the hotel for business at 745 AM and don't get back before 530 or 6PM. That's the reason I called Mr. Kensedder last night. You were already off duty. I only asked Mr. Kensedder if he could do anything about those little bars of soap.

The new maid you assigned me must have thought I was a new check-in today, since she left another 3 bars of hotel soap in my medicine cabinet along with her regular delivery of 3 bars on the bathroom shelf. In just 5 days here I have accumulated 24 little bars of soap. Why are you doing this to me?

S. Berman

Dear Mr. Berman, Your maid, Kathy, has been instructed to stop delivering soap to your room and remove the extra soaps. If I can be of further assistance, please call extension 1108 between 8AM and 5PM. Thank you.

Elaine Carmen, Housekeeper

Dear Mr. Kensedder, My bath-size Dial is missing. Every bar of soap was taken from my room including my own bath-size Dial. I came in late last night and had to call the bellhop to bring me 4 little Cashmere Bouquets.

S. Berman

Dear Mr. Berman, I have informed our housekeeper, Elaine Carmen, of your soap problem. I cannot understand why there was no soap in your room since our maids are instructed to leave 3 bars of soap each time they service a room.

The situation will be rectified immediately. Please accept my apologies for the inconvenience.

Martin L. Kensedder, Assistant Manager

Dear Mrs. Carmen, WHO ON EARTH WAS POSSESSED TO LEAVE 54 little bars of Camay in my room!?! I came in last night and found 54 little bars of soap. I don't want 54 little bars of Camay. I want my one blessed bar of bath-size Dial. Do you realize I have 54 bars of soap in here! All I want is my bath-size Dial. Please give me back my bath-size Dial.

S. Berman

Dear Mr. Berman, You complained of too much soap in your room so I had them removed. Then you complained to Mr. Kensedder that all your soap was missing so I personally returned them. The 24 Camays which had been taken and the 3 Camays you are supposed to receive daily (sic). I don't know anything about the 4 Cashmere Bouquets. Obviously your maid, Kathy, did not know I had returned your soaps so she also brought 24 Camays plus the 3 daily Camays. I don't know where you got the idea this hotel issues bath-size Dial. I was able to locate some bath-size Ivory that I left in your room.

Elaine Carmen, Housekeeper

Dear Mrs. Carmen, Just a short note to bring you up-to-date on my latest soap inventory.

As of today I possess:

- On shelf under medicine cabinet - 18 Camay in 4 stacks of 4 and 1 stack of 2.

- On Kleenex dispenser - 11 Camay in 2 stacks of 4 and 1 stack of 3.

- On bedroom dresser - 1 stack of 3 Cashmere Bouquet, 1 stack of 4 hotel-size Ivory, and 8 Camay in 2 stacks of 4.

- Inside medicine cabinet - 14 Camay in 3 stacks of 4 and 1 stack of 2.

- In shower soap dish - 6 Camay, very moist.

- On northeast corner of tub - 1 Cashmere Bouquet, slightly used.

- On northwest corner of tub - 6 Camays in 2 stacks of 3.

Please ask Kathy when she services my room to make sure the stacks are neatly piled and dusted. Also, please advise her that stacks of more than 4 have a tendency to tip. May I suggest that my bedroom windowsill is not in use and will make an excellent spot for future soap deliveries.

One more item, I have purchased another bar of bath-sized Dial which I am keeping in the hotel vault in order to avoid further misunderstandings.

S. Berman

Thanks for Laughing.

- Pastor Tim

ISBN 155369030-3

9 781553 690306